Policy Papers
in International Affairs

NUMBER 26

# Why We Still Need the United Nations

THE COLLECTIVE MANAGEMENT OF
INTERNATIONAL CONFLICT, 1945-1984

## Ernst B. Haas

Institute of
International Studies
UNIVERSITY OF CALIFORNIA • BERKELEY

*In sponsoring the Policy Papers in International Affairs series, the Institute of International Studies reasserts its commitment to a vigorous policy debate by providing a forum for innovative approaches to important policy issues. The views expressed in each paper are those of the author only, and publication in this series does not constitute endorsement by the Institute.*

International Standard Book Number 0-87725-526-1

Library of Congress Catalog Card Number 86-84126

© 1986 by the Regents of the University of California

## CONTENTS

*List of Tables* vi

*List of Figures* vii

*Acknowledgments* ix

INTRODUCTION 1

I. THE UNITED NATIONS CHARTER AND THE POSTWAR CONCERT OF POWER 4

II. HOW TO STUDY THE IMPACT OF THE UNITED NATIONS 8

III. CORRELATES OF UNITED NATIONS SUCCESS AND FAILURE 22

IV. WHY MILITARY OPERATIONS ARE USUALLY SUCCESSFUL 35

V. COULD THINGS BE BETTER? 54

APPENDIXES

A. Referrals of International Disputes, 1945-1984 73

B. Correlates of Success in United Nations Disputes 95

## LIST OF TABLES

1. REFERRALS OF ALL DISPUTES INVOLVING MILITARY OPERATIONS AND FIGHTING — 19
2. REFERRALS OF SERIOUS DISPUTES INVOLVING MILITARY OPERATIONS AND FIGHTING — 20
3. ATTRIBUTES OF REFERRED AND NONREFERRED DISPUTES AS OF 1980 — 21
4. INCIDENCE OF RESOURCE-RELATED DISPUTES BY DECADES, 1945-1984 — 26
5. UNITED NATIONS SUCCESS IN MANAGING POLITICAL ISSUES — 30
6. COMPARISON OF DISPUTES REFERRED TO UN AND REGIONALS — 33
7. MANDATES OF UNITED NATIONS MILITARY OPERATIONS — 38
8. CONTEXT OF UNITED NATIONS MILITARY OPERATIONS — 40
9. THE VETO AND UN SUCCESS — 44

### Appendix A

DISPUTES REFERRED TO THE UNITED NATIONS — 73

DISPUTES REFERRED TO THE LEAGUE OF ARAB STATES — 82

DISPUTES REFERRED TO THE ORGANIZATION OF AMERICAN STATES (OAS) — 84

DISPUTES REFERRED TO THE ORGANIZATION OF AFRICAN UNITY (OAU) — 86

DISPUTES REFERRED TO THE COUNCIL OF EUROPE — 87

DISPUTES WITH MILITARY OPERATIONS NOT REFERRED TO MAJOR INTERNATIONAL ORGANIZATIONS — 88

## Appendix B

| | |
|---|---|
| A. CORRELATES OF SUCCESS: UNITED NATIONS | 96 |
| B. SALIENCE OF UNITED NATIONS DISPUTES | 98 |
| C. GLOBAL CONTEXT OF UNITED NATIONS DISPUTES | 99 |
| D. MANAGEMENT OF UNITED NATIONS DISPUTES | 100 |
| E. CORRELATES OF GREAT SUCCESS BY ERA | 101 |
| F. CORRELATES OF LIMITED SUCCESS BY ERA | 102 |
| G. NONIMPLEMENTERS OF SUBSTANTIVE UNITED NATIONS DECISIONS | 103 |

## LIST OF FIGURES

| | |
|---|---|
| 1. SUCCESS BY ERA: REFERRALS AND IMPACTS | 15 |
| 2. SUCCESS BY ERA: PERCENT OF ALL IMPACTS | 16 |
| 3. UNITED NATIONS – DIMENSIONS OF FAILURE: PERCENTAGE OF DISPUTES LACKING ANY IMPACT | 18 |
| 4. REGIONAL ORGANIZATIONS – DIMENSIONS OF FAILURE: PERCENTAGE OF DISPUTES LACKING ANY IMPACT | 18 |
| 5. SALIENCE OF UNITED NATIONS DISPUTES AND OVERALL SUCCESS | 25 |
| 6. TYPES OF DISPUTES AND OVERALL SUCCESS | 25 |
| 7. UNITED NATIONS: TYPES OF DECISIONS AND OPERATIONS | 28 |
| 8. UNITED NATIONS: TYPES OF LEADERSHIP AND CONSENSUS | 28 |
| 9. NONIMPLEMENTERS OF SUBSTANTIVE UN DECISIONS | 64 |

## ACKNOWLEDGMENTS

I am indebted to Jacqueline Reich, Daniel Verdier, and Benny Miller for research assistance, and to Robert L. Butterworth for sharing an unpublished manuscript with me. Portions of this study were previously published as "Regime Decay: Conflict Management and International Organizations, 1945-1981" in *International Organization,* 37:2, Spring 1983, reprinted by permission of the MIT Press. The study was originally commissioned by the United Nations Institute for Training and Research for its project on the Maintenance of International Peace and Security. I am grateful to Mark Zacher for a careful reading of the manuscript, but I alone am responsible for any remaining ambiguities or errors.

E. B. H.

*Berkeley, California*
*March 1986*

## INTRODUCTION

There is a widespread impression that collective conflict management by international organizations has failed. Such a judgment is simplistic and misleading. Failure as compared to what? Is there more intolerable conflict today than in 1950 or 1970? Are noninstitutionalized modes of conflict management more successful than the efforts of international organizations? To attribute failure to the United Nations and to regional organizations is to endow these entities with a degree of autonomy they do not possess. The organizations cannot fail, but their members can behave in such a fashion as to impede the realization of rules of conduct enshrined in their charters.

But should we blame a leopard for having spots? The superpowers are often blamed for ignoring the United Nations and for causing disputes which are ultimately dealt with by hortatory and ineffectual UN resolutions. Respect for the UN is said to be low because words, repeated ad nauseam, take the place of action. States of all kinds are accused of ignoring the machinery for the peaceful settlement of disputes and preferring to confront each other outside international forums. All of these charges are correct—but beside the point.

We must remind ourselves that collective conflict management is an aspect of foreign policy; it does not replace foreign policy. Diplomacy and action in an international organization provide one way of implementing foreign policy. Far from transcending the objectives that states consider to be their national interests, conflict management organizations are forums for realizing these interests when action outside the organizations is either not possible or not desired. Action by the organizations does not monopolize the possibilities open to states; action outside them usually is possible and is often preferred. To fail, one must be empowered to act autonomously. Few modern international organizations have this capacity. None in the present study do. Judging the record of the UN, the Organization of American States (OAS), the Arab League, and the Organization for African Unity (OAU) requires an understanding of the behavior of the member states toward each other.

I shall review this behavior since the inception of each organization by seeking to answer the following questions:

1. What has been the impact of each organization on the disputes referred to it? Have disputes been settled, or merely abated and perhaps isolated? Under what conditions have hostilities been stopped?
2. What percentage of disputes has been referred to international organizations instead of being managed by other means? Is there a tendency toward more or less conflict management outside international organizations?
3. To what extent is conflict management dominated by two meta-issues: the cold war and the decolonization struggle? Is conflict over physical resources emerging as an additional meta-issue? Is there a trend away from domination by any meta-issue? Does it matter whether the parties to a dispute are members of the same alliance or are nonaligned?
4. Are disputes among states becoming more or less intense? Is the incidence of warfare increasing or decreasing? Are disputes more localized or do they spread more readily? How do the disputes referred to international organizations fit into these trends?
5. What has been the pattern of organization action in the face of various kinds of disputes? Have decisions become more or less forceful? Has consensus been weaker or stronger? Have mediatory, supervisory, and peacekeeping operations been mounted less or more frequently over time, and with what results?
6. What kinds of disputes can be handled effectively with military operations launched by international organizations, and what kinds cannot?
7. On balance, have international organizations made international relations more peaceful, or have they sometimes exacerbated international tensions?
8. Do regional organizations and the UN complement each other's work or complicate it?

Answers to these questions constitute a commentary on how modern states cope with the most extreme and the most salient grievances they have toward each other, but they tell us little about the kinds of aspirations states entertain with respect to a particular world order. The UN Charter was certainly intended by its framers as a statement of aspirations about the future shape of the world and the rules that ought to govern conduct in it. We must look at these aspirations and rules in order to appreciate whether and to what degree the conflict and conflict management behavior of states has departed from them.

# I

# THE UNITED NATIONS CHARTER AND THE POSTWAR CONCERT OF POWER

Designing an organization presupposes a vision of a desirable order. The designers of international organizations usually seek to fashion a world order that will be able to avoid the causes of the troubles the world has just survived. The League of Nations was built on the principle of collective security because the authors of the Covenant attributed World War I to the principle of antagonistic alliances and the faulty mechanism of the balance of power. The authors of the UN Charter, on the other hand, were preoccupied with the conditions that brought Hitler to power and with the context that induced him to attempt the conquest of Europe. They credited the defeat of the Axis to the strength of their alliance, and the world order they aimed at took for granted that the alliance could also guarantee the peace of the future, provided the conditions that were thought to have caused Germany and Japan to behave as they did could be avoided. While the statesmen of 1919 thought that the immediate causes of World War I—the quarrel between Austria and Serbia and the absence of collective institutions for peacefully settling disputes among states—should not be permitted to recur, the statesmen of 1945 were more impressed with the need for military might for buttressing institutions devoted to peaceful settlement. These differences illustrate a major conundrum of world order design: Are the chief causes of war to be found in deep-seated prior conditions (usually referred to as the underlying causes) or the immediate circumstances that dominated the decisions that led to the outbreak of war? Few doubt that both are important, but, as we shall see, it may be impossible to design organizations that address both with equal success.

Underlying conditions include the sources of deep dissatisfaction with the status quo: unrequited nationalist aspirations, perceptions of long-lived military threats, ideological incompatibilities, demands for economic resources. Immediate causes have to do with the perception—or misperception—of an antagonist's military moves, the interpretation of his motives, the assessment of his will to fight or willingness to negotiate. They also involve the atmosphere during a crisis, the pressure of time, the felt need to be decisive, the ability to control remote military actions from the capital, the capacity to escalate or deescalate so as to support diplomatic moves and avoid hostilities.

The means chosen to eliminate the two types of causes differ enormously. Debate still rages over whether the major wars of the twentieth century are to be attributed primarily to the underlying or to the immediate causes.* The authors of the UN Charter assumed that the underlying causes were to be eliminated by the victorious powers acting alone or in concert with each other outside the UN; they gave the UN a very weak mandate for dealing with them. But they conferred a strong mandate on the UN for making permanent the order decided on outside the UN by so designing the rules as to enable it to deal with immediate causes. Eliminating the underlying causes involves notions of justice and of peaceful change, but avoiding the immediate causes, once the general lines of the postwar order were decreed, involved only institutionalized procedures for dealing with specific disputes.

The drafters of the Charter could have proposed a world organization with autonomous powers of a supranational character, but they chose instead to sanctify the principles of nationalism and state sovereignty. The organization they created is only a confederation of juridical equals, united in almost permanent conference. They could have created an order of widespread equal rights and equal participation by all states, large and small; they opted instead for an oligarchy of the powerful. The procedures for dealing with disputes, for maintaining and enforcing the rules of the new order were all but monopolized in the Charter by the oligarchic Security Council.

The Charter's world order was dedicated to the preservation of the new status quo. The five permanent members of the Security Council had to sanction all action; their failure to agree meant

---

*For very instructive discussions of the relative roles of underlying and immediate causes of war as systematic explanations of why wars occur, see Glen H. Snyder and Paul Diesing, *Conflict Among Nations* (Princeton: Princeton University Press, 1977), and Richard Ned Lebow, *Between Peace and War* (Baltimore: Johns Hopkins University Press, 1981). Both books show the interaction between both types and a tendency for immediate causes to explain outcomes more persuasively than underlying causes. As we shall see, this is good news for collective conflict management.

inaction. They alone were to enforce the norms. This implied—since each had a veto—either that they were expected to be in agreement on almost everything or that they would keep disputes among themselves off the agenda and confine the UN caseload to disputes of no great salience in their foreign policies. In short, the United Nations under the aegis of the concert assumed consensus on world order issues among the permanent members. With the advent of the cold war and bipolarity as a fact of life, none of these assumptions and conditions remained relevant. If new norms and rules had not been invented after 1947, the cold war would have condemned the United Nations to death then and there.

Provisions dealing with bringing about peaceful change of the status quo became the business of the "democratic" General Assembly, but its resolutions, unlike those of the Security Council, were only recommendations. The General Assembly was to undertake studies of situations likely to lead to war, to concern itself with the emancipation of colonial territories, and to deal with aspects of international economic relations that might constitute underlying causes of interstate conflict. Interstate disputes were within its mandate when they were not on the agenda of the Security Council—subject to the rule that its resolutions were recommendations only. The preservation of the status quo was clearly favored over the provision for peaceful change.

The principle of the big power concert was breached in some respects. Alliances among states were not forbidden, although the principle of the concert is inconsistent with bloc formation. Regional organizations (the only ones in existence in 1945 were American- and British-led alliances) were to get first crack at regional disputes, subject to the supremacy of UN norms. The self-defense clause (Article 51) provided an escape hatch for extra-UN military action which was an invitation to proceed outside the concert. Relations with Japan and Germany were reserved to the major powers, who were thus able to include the defeated powers in new regional and/or self-defense provisions (as they proceeded to do after 1948). The only concessions to supranationality in the Charter are the power of the Secretary-General to call threatening situations to the attention of the Security Council, the principle of obligatory financial contributions to the UN budget decided by majority vote, and the duty of the Security Council to enforce decisions of the International Court of Justice.

Thus the dice were loaded to favor the status quo created by the big victors. The lacunae in the new rules could be interpreted as favoring the hegemony of the biggest of the victors—the United States. Elimination of the underlying causes of conflict was neglected; methods for avoiding the immediate causes were emphasized. Neither the speed of the movement for decolonization nor the trend toward new tight and antagonistic alliances was foreseen. Why did they not make a shambles of the UN early in its life?*

The story of the drafting of the Charter and the principle of the concert remind us that the context that shapes state behavior is intrinsic to the functioning of the UN. The eventual adaptation of Charter principles to the new realities of a world dominated by cold war-related alliances and the pressure to end colonial rule shows that the initial context is not the final word in the life cycle of organizations. State behavior changes, and as it changes it seeks to adapt international organizations to its new purposes. If the member states show a semblance of reciprocity to each other's desires, a willingness to grant the other's interests and to forego immediate benefits in the hope of a later reward, new norms and rules can take the place of the ones discredited by new aspirations and configurations. Provisions for peaceful change and concern for eliminating the underlying causes of war may yet come to the fore in collective conflict management. After the disintegration of the postwar concert, adaptation in the UN took the form of "permissive enforcement with balancing," which dominated the organization's conflict management activity from 1948 until 1955 under the hegemony of the United States. After 1955 the anticolonial revolt joined to the continuing cold war resulted in a new adaptation I label "permissive engagement," which was practiced until the late 1960s. (Both adaptations are discussed in detail in part IV below.) Since that time few new adaptations are discernible, though the earlier ones have not been discarded. The overall effectiveness of the UN in conflict management has declined. Now our task is to account for the early successes and the later failures, and to speculate on the possibility of new adaptations in the future.

*A look at the UN record in conflict management during the concert years is instructive. Of eleven disputes referred to the UN between 1945 and 1947, no impact was scored on six. All six involved challenges to the territorial and ideological status quo. Five disputes were managed or moderated with some success, including two (the Corfu Channel and Azerbaijan) that pitted the United States against the Soviet Union. The remaining three dealt with postcolonial issues on which the major powers were in agreement. The concert did function, if somewhat haphazardly.

## II

## HOW TO STUDY THE IMPACT OF
## THE UNITED NATIONS

This study of the United Nations draws on "disputes" that occurred between July 1945 and September 1984.* What is a dispute? A dispute is a specific grievance between two or more states about a specific subject involving an allegation that a provision of the UN Charter or a major resolution of an authoritative UN organ has been violated. Typically they involve accusations of aggression or armed attack, claims to or seizures of territory, intervention in a civil war, violations of human rights, a demand for independence. Imperialism and nationalism, the cold war, racism, and the arms race are not disputes in this sense. To be sure, they may be the basic conditions that provoke the disputes. It may well be true that unless the provisions for peaceful change written into the Charter are taken seriously, the specific disputes will continue to occur. On the other hand, it remains to be seen if disputes that can be traced back to

---

*Robert L. Butterworth, Joseph S. Nye, and I created the data set for the period 1945-70, reporting it in Haas, Butterworth, and Nye, *Conflict Management by International Organizations* (Morristown, N.J.: General Learning Press, 1972). The definition of "dispute," the specification of variables used in the analysis, and the coding procedures are described there and in Ernst B. Haas, "Regime Decay: Conflict Management and International Organizations, 1945-1981," *International Organization* (Spring 1983): 236-41. I used the same definitions and procedures in this study. Data for the period 1971-78 were taken from Robert L. Butterworth, *Managing Interstate Conflict* (Pittsburgh: University Center for International Studies, University of Pittsburgh, 1976) and from Butterworth's unpublished manuscript "Managing International Conflict" (1980). I am responsible for preparing data for the period since 1978 and for any mistakes in coding and interpretation throughout. Disputes are credited to the five-year period during which they were first referred to an organization, and are counted only once, even if they remained on the agenda during subsequent periods and even if success came about in a later period. Certain long-lived disputes were broken up according to coding rules described in Haas, Butterworth, and Nye—notably those between Israel and the Arab states, the Kashmir dispute, and the situation in South Africa. Butterworth compared computations

colonialism or the cold war have consistently been excluded from conflict management in deference to the Charter's bias in favor of the status quo. Whether the Charter bias against peaceful change has seriously hampered the work of the UN is an empirical question we must investigate. In any event, whether or not a dispute has its basis in some important underlying condition of international politics, its surface manifestations still involve the proximate causes of conflict and are still subject to the procedures for peaceful settlement. If we account properly for the world political context in which conflict management is attempted, we can still "catch" what went on, and if we code the behavior of states appropriately, we can stilll draw conclusions about the ability of the UN to deal with underlying as well as proximate causes of conflict.

We found a total of 319 disputes between 1945 and 1984. Of these, 96 were not referred to any international organization, 137 made the agenda of the UN, 30 were referred to the OAS, 27 to the OAU, 24 to the Arab League, and 5 to the Council of Europe. Since it was impossible to construct a full universe of all nonreferred disputes, this set includes only disputes in which at least some fighting occurred. Double counting exists in the sense that 22 disputes were referred both to the UN and to a regional organization and 3 disputes were referred both to the OAU and the Arab League.

---

of success based on the present method with the alternative of crediting success to the period in which it actually occurred. He found that the two curves were hardly distinguishable.

I excluded disputes in which no management action was possible since there was nothing for the organization to do short of enforcement. In other instances the parties appealed to the organization for propaganda reasons only and expected no action. Examples of excluded disputes are the Eichmann abduction and various airplane incidents pitting the United States against the USSR. There were 22 excluded disputes for the United Nations, 4 for the regionals. The disputes in the study are distributed as follows:

|  | Referred to United Nations | Referred to Regionals | Nonreferred | Total |
| --- | --- | --- | --- | --- |
| Involved military operations | 100 | 56 | 96 | 252 |
| No military operations | 37 | 30 | -- | 67 |
| *Total* | 137 | 86 | 96 | 319 |

## GLOBAL CONTEXT OF DISPUTES

The contextual features for which we have to watch out are given by the core theoretical assumptions we all make about world politics. The relative power of the antagonists, their position in alliances, and the underlying issue that engages them (if any) are assumed to influence everyone's options and sharply constrain choice. Disputes are referred to international organizations by a complainant so that he may "win"; the respondent is concerned with "not losing." Mediators may regard a dispute as generally threatening world peace and therefore desire to dampen it without designating winners and losers, but the primary parties regard their conflict as a zero-sum game.

Each party to a dispute is ranked on a scale of power running from superpower to the weakest states, with large and middle powers as intermediate ranks. The United States, following the breakdown of the post-1945 concert of power, was the hegemon until the middle of the 1960s; thereafter, its automatic two-thirds majority in the General Assembly evaporated. No new hegemonic state took its place, but whenever the members of the Non-Aligned Movement voted together, they dominated the organization from that date on. The Soviet Union has never occupied the hegemon's seat; its influence outside the Security Council is felt when it energetically asssociates itself with the bloc of the Non-Aligned.

Since the UN is the mirror, not the shaper, of world politics, it necessarily reflects alliances, blocs, and alignments that exist outside it. How these, in turn, constrain conflict management remains to be seen. Each dispute is coded with respect to the alignment of the parties. The parties may be allied with each other either because they belong to the same collective self-defense pact or because they have military and political understandings with the leaders of these pacts. The parties may also belong to opposing alliances. One party may be allied while the other is nonaligned, or both parties may be nonaligned.

How can we characterize the issues embedded in a dispute? First of all, I stipulate the existence of two meta-issues: the cold war and the decolonization process. Nineteen percent of all disputes were clearly manifestations of the global struggle between the American and Soviet-led alliances, at least as perceived by the two bloc leaders. Another 20 percent were outgrowths of the decolonization struggle, or manifestations of the nationalism of the colonized.

While such disputes may also contain a cold war dimension, the coding concentrates on the colonial aspect. That leaves 61 percent which were not connected with either meta-issue. Often such disputes are "postcolonial," in the sense that the conflict is over territory previously ruled by one or more empires, which upon withdrawing failed to designate a successor generally recognized as legitimate within agreed boundaries. Since the disputants are the successor states, however, and not the erstwhile imperialist, such disputes are considered as part of the postcolonial context. I further distinguish between interstate and internal conflicts. Civil wars, in order to qualify for this study, must be characterized by the actual or alleged intervention of an outside state. Such disputes may be local manifestations of the cold war, or they may be unrelated to any meta-issue. Civil wars account for 31 percent of all disputes; 27 percent of them were cold war-related while 73 percent were not.

Some commentators believe that a new meta-issue has emerged, a new underlying condition that spawns international conflict— i.e., disputes about such natural resources as oil, minerals, food, access to waterways and fisheries. A resource meta-issue may overlap with cold war and decolonization conflicts, or it may appear as an unrelated issue. We shall see whether a recoding of disputes along these lines results in the emergence of a new underlying source of conflict.

TRIVIAL AND THREATENING DISPUTES

Not every dispute brought to an international organization really threatens world peace—unless we take the old nostrum about the indivisibility of peace very literally. Disputes differ in their intensity, the extent to which they have escalated beyond the primary parties, and the extent and the purposes that characterize hostilities. The intensity of each dispute is coded in terms of its duration, the number of fatalities, and the likelihood of its escalating in the absence of attempted organizational management.

Several degrees of fighting are possible. Each dispute is coded as to whether there were any hostilities at all, whether the fighting is mere skirmishing designed to frighten an antagonist, whether the fighting consists of military operations supportive of diplomatic efforts, or whether the intent of the operation is to defeat the enemy and seize his territory.

Finally, the geographic scope of the dispute must be ascertained. Some disputes remain purely bilateral. Others escalate into situations in which one or both of the parties receive military and diplomatic support from third parties, although the supporting states are not willing to fight. A further escalation results when neighboring states are willing to enter the conflict militarily. The final escalation occurs when states external to the region enter the fighting actively.

## MANAGED AND UNMANAGED DISPUTES

Managing a dispute involves making collective decisions, mounting field operations, exercising leadership, and building consensus. Decisions vary from minimal discussion that does not lead to the adoption of a resolution or shifts the dispute to another organization, through a resolution that does not call for action (i.e., an essentially rhetorical statement), to a resolution that calls for operations of some kind. Operations, in turn, cover a wide spectrum— from none being authorized, through fact-finding, mediation, and conciliation, which involve missions ranging from one to perhaps twenty people, to truce-observation, peacekeeping, and enforcement measures, which involve—at the extreme—entire armies. Resolutions have to be sponsored, advocated, and supported in order to be adopted. I determined whether leadership in these activities was exercised by one superpower, jointly by both superpowers, by a large power, or by middle, small, or smallest states. I also determined whether leadership was exercised by the Secretary-General or the presiding officer of the Security Council, either acting alone or jointly with a member government. The consensus variable codes the vote by which the strongest winning resolution was adopted. Possibilities range from no consensus, through the bare satisfaction of the constitutional voting requirement, to a generous margin beyond the minimal requirement, to near-unanimity.

Conflict may be successfully managed in various ways. I label these "abatement," "isolation," "settlement," and "stopping hostilities." Every dispute is capable of being settled and abated, but not every dispute was judged likely to escalate beyond the initial parties, and obviously hostilities could not be stopped if the dispute did not involve any fighting. Each dispute was scored on whether the organization was somewhat successful on each of the dimensions applicable to the dispute, whether it scored a great impact, or whether no impact of any kind was discernible. A score of one hundred means that the organization made a major contribution on all applicable dimensions during the period in question; a score of zero means that not even limited impact on a single dimension could be observed.

Judgments were made by ascertaining the degree of compliance with attempts on the part of the organization to manage a conflict. The organization is given full credit for "settling" a dispute if the final outcome reflects, in essence, the content of the applicable resolutions; it is given limited credit if some of the intent of the resolutions is adopted by the parties. If the parties observe a cease-fire ordered by the UN, the organization is given full credit for "stopping hostilities"; if the cease-fire is obeyed sporadically, limited credit is given. If member states, after being called upon to aid in a settlement, refrain from aiding one or both of the parties, the organization receives full credit for "isolating" the dispute; if some members obey and others continue to side with one of the disputants, limited credit is given. "Abating" a dispute involves the slackening of hostilities, the cessation of intervention or propaganda, the scaling down of rival claims, the initiation of negotiations, or the acceptance of third-party intercession. When all of these steps are taken in response to organizational initiatives, full credit is given; if some of these measures are adopted, limited credit is given.*

SUCCESS IS RELATIVE

The trend of organizational success in managing disputes is shown in Figures 1 and 2. The UN's overall score is 23, as compared to 32 for the OAS, 18 for the OAU, 19 for the Arab League, and

---

*The formula for calculating organizational impact for each dispute is as follows:

A. *Success in stopping hostilities*
   n = No opportunity to stop through no fault of organization
   0 = Failed to stop
   1 = Helped to stop
   2 = Stopped

B. *Success in conflict abatement for three years*
   0 = Failed to abate
   1 = Helped to abate
   2 = Abated

18 for the Council of Europe. The picture shows a decline in effectiveness for the UN and the regionals. The success curves, in general, follow the curve for referrals, thus showing that organizational load remains roughly proportional to organizational impact. However, the UN has scored fewer and fewer great impacts since 1965, thus lending some credence to U Thant's exaggerated prediction that "the UN has ten years to become effective or disappear."*  The regionals imitated the trend after 1975. Yet—and this is perhaps a more important finding—both continue to score limited impacts, and the decline of the regionals has been less steep than the UN's.

---

C. *Success in conflict settlement*
    0 = Failed to settle
    1 = Helped to settle
    2 = Settled

D. *Success in isolating conflict*
    n = Conflict had no opportunity to expand
    0 = Failed to isolate
    1 = Helped to isolate
    2 = Isolated

*Formula for computing success:* $A + B + C + D = raw\ success\ (maximum = 8)$

### Success Scale

| | |
|---|---|
| *None* | Organizational action made no difference to outcome on any dimension (0 raw score) |
| *Some, limited* | Organizational action made some difference on one or two dimensions (one or two 1 scores; raw score of 1 or 2) |
| *Great* | Organizational action made some difference on three or four dimensions (three or four 1 scores; raw score of 3 or 4) |
| | Organizational action made a great difference on at least one dimension plus at least some difference on one other (one or more 2 scores + one, two, or three 1 scores; one or two 2 scores + not more than two $n$ scores; one 2 score plus one 1 score, plus 0s or $n$s; raw score of 3, 4, 5, 6, 7, 8) |

An organizational score of 100 in each era means that the organization achieved a score of 6, 7, or 8 for *each* dispute.

---

*Cited in Lester B. Pearson, The UN at 25," *Saturday Review* (6/27/70): 16. The low scores in the period since 1980 are probably temporary since impacts may be scored in disputes referred during this period at a later time. In all previous studies using this mode of measurement, the most recent era always scored poorest, only

THE IMPACT OF THE UNITED NATIONS 15

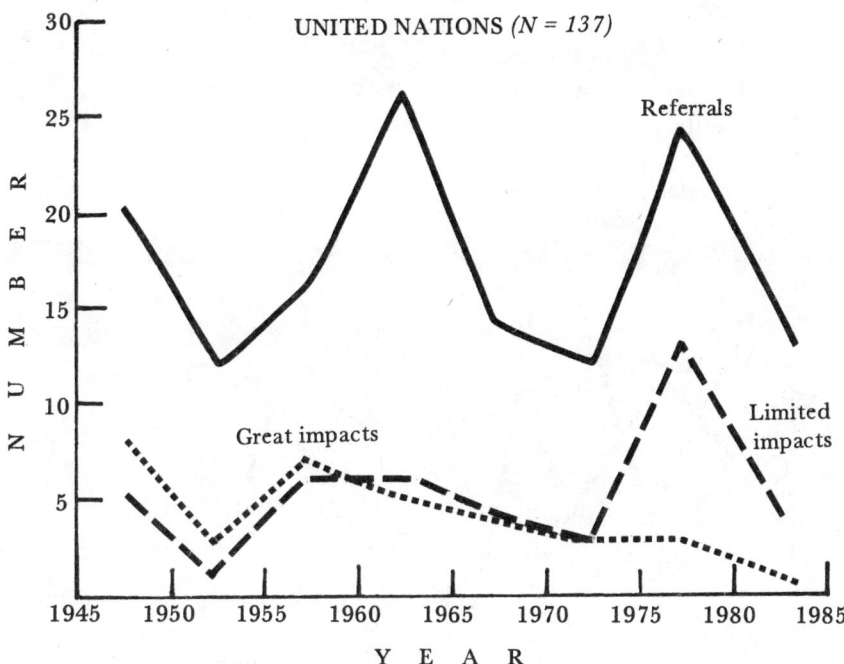

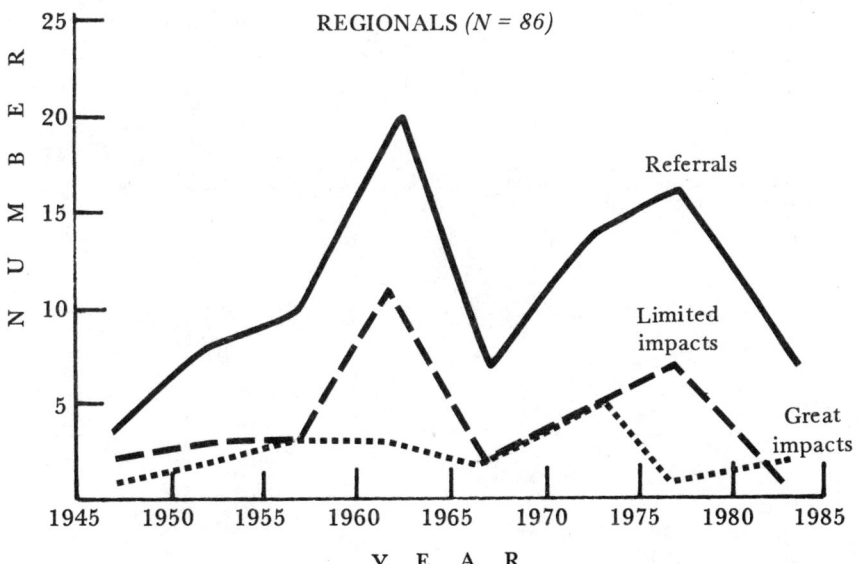

Figure 1. SUCCESS BY ERA: REFERRALS AND IMPACTS

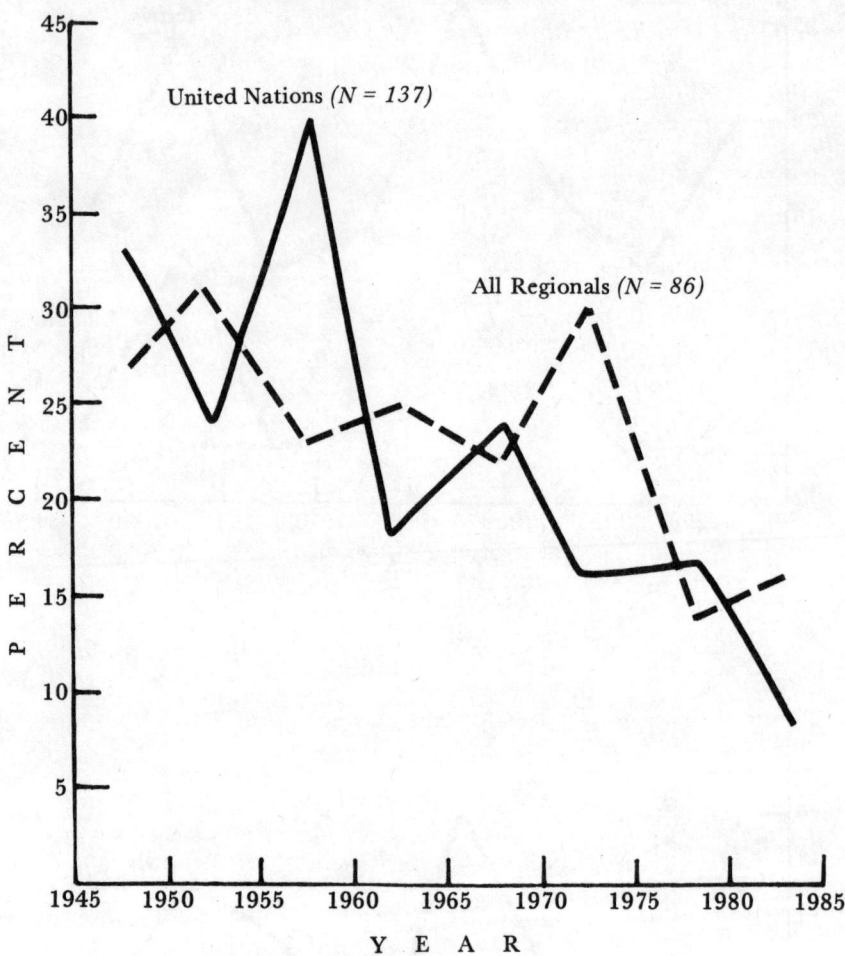

Figure 2. SUCCESS BY ERA: PERCENT OF ALL IMPACTS

Failure on one dimension and overall decline do *not* imply failure on all dimensions, as shown in Figures 3 and 4.* Neither the UN nor the regionals have successfully stopped ongoing hostilities with any consistency since the early 1960s.† The record of both with respect to settling disputes has almost always been dismal. The UN's early successes on this dimension were confined to cases of relatively amiable decolonization.** When it comes to isolating disputes, however, the picture gets more complex. During the 1960s and the early 1970s, the regionals were quite effective in keeping disputes from spreading. Since 1980 they again show some ability

---

to pick up slightly when the data were reexamined five years later. The improvements never sufficed to change the overall trend, however. The number and percentage of nonreferred disputes in the most recent era may also contain a distortion. While these disputes were not yet referred, it frequently happens that referral occurs in a subsequent era if no early solution is found by the parties themselves.

*The 40-years scores of failure on all dimensions are (in percent):

|  | United Nations | Regionals |
|---|---|---|
| Failed to abate | 47% | 44% |
| Failed to stop hostilities | 63 | 63 |
| Failed to isolate | 66 | 55 |
| Failed to settle | 75 | 74 |

†Cases of "great" UN success in stopping hostilities: Korean negotiations (1951-53), West Irian, Zaire independence, Cyprus civil war, Shatt-el-Arab (1975). Cases of "limited" UN success in stopping hostilities: Indonesian independence, Greek civil war, Palestine independence, Kashmir secession, Palestine truce (1949-56), Kashmir negotiations (1949-64), KMT troops in Burma, Algerian independence, Suez war, Palestine borders (1957-67), Sakiet raid, Lebanon/Jordan civil war, Laos civil war (1959-62), Bizerta, Aden independence, Cambodian border (1964-67), second Kashmir war, Six-Day war, Yom Kippur war, raids on Angola, Litani River war, Israeli raids on Lebanon (1979-82), New Hebrides independence, mining of Corinto.

**Cases of "great" UN success in settling disputes: Indonesian independence, British Togoland, status of Cyrenaica, KMT troops in Burma, status of West Irian, Suez war, British Cameroon, Thai/Cambodia border (1960), Zaire independence, status of African High Commission Territories, status of Ifni. Cases of "limited" UN success in settling disputes: Azerbaijan, French withdrawal from Levant, Palestine independence, Kashmir secession, Russian wives, Korean negotiations (1951-53), China Seas piracy, Sakiet raid, Wadi Halfa, Lebanon/Jordan civil war (1958), Bizerta, Sarawak/Sabah, Aden independence, Cyprus civil war (1963-73), Rhodesian independence, second Kashmir war, Djibouti independence, Shatt-el-Arab (1969-75), Equatorial Guinea independence, Bahrein independence, Burmese refugees, New Hebrides independence, Afghanistan (?).

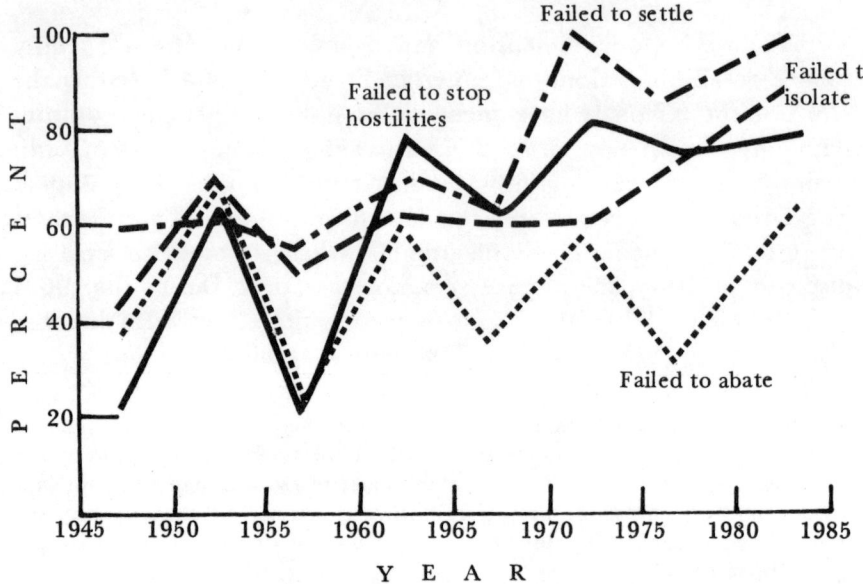

Figure 3. UNITED NATIONS – DIMENSIONS OF FAILURE:
PERCENTAGE OF DISPUTES LACKING ANY IMPACT
*(N = 137)*

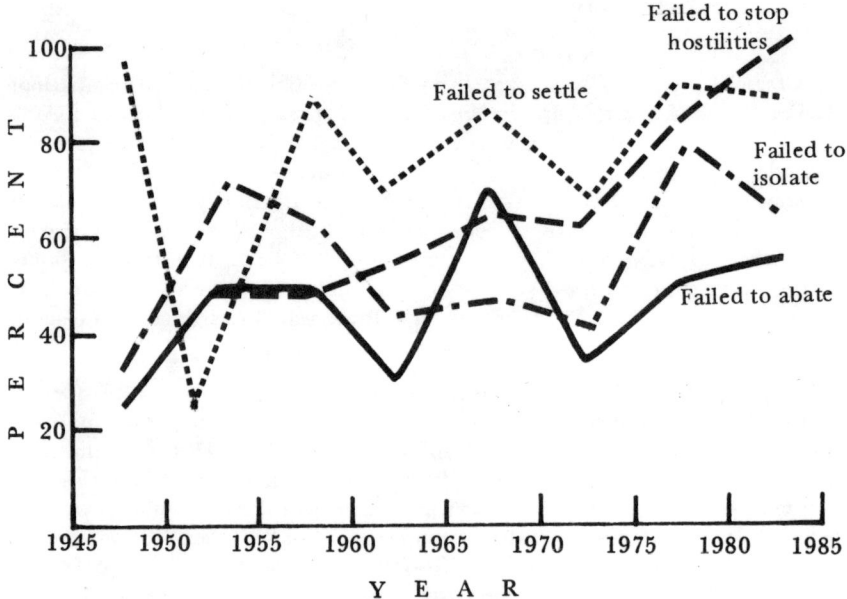

Figure 4. REGIONAL ORGANIZATIONS – DIMENSIONS OF FAILURE:
PERCENTAGE OF DISPUTES LACKING ANY IMPACT
*(N = 86)*

to score isolating impacts. The UN's record, by contrast, matches the overall decline on the other dimensions noted by U Thant.* The exception to all these findings is the abatement of disputes, admittedly the simplest of the conflict management tasks. Both the UN and the regionals have always been most effective on this dimension and continue to be so. It is simply not true that the UN has lost all relevance with respect to conflict management. Even since its drastic downturn in the early 1960s, the organization succeeds in abating about half of the disputes referred to it.

IS THE UN BECOMING IRRELEVANT?

But it has been said that the UN is losing relevance in another sense: fewer and fewer of the more serious disputes are referred to it for management. This claim too is inaccurate (see Table 1). The

Table 1
REFERRALS OF ALL DISPUTES INVOLVING MILITARY OPERATIONS AND FIGHTING

| Era | Total Number | To United Nations | | To Regionals | | Nonreferred | |
|---|---|---|---|---|---|---|---|
| | | Number | Percent | Number | Percent | Number | Percent |
| 1945-50 | 24 | 10 | 42% | 1 | 4% | 13 | 54% |
| 1951-55 | 20 | 9 | 45 | 4 | 20 | 7 | 35 |
| 1956-60 | 26 | 9 | 35 | 5 | 19 | 12 | 46 |
| 1961-65 | 49 | 21 | 43 | 15 | 30 | 13 | 27 |
| 1966-70 | 21 | 12 | 57 | 4 | 19 | 5 | 24 |
| 1971-75 | 25 | 8 | 32 | 8 | 32 | 9 | 36 |
| 1976-80 | 41 | 16 | 39 | 10 | 24 | 15 | 37 |
| 1981-84 | 38 | 12 | 32 | 5 | 13 | 21 | 55 |
| 1945-84 | 244 | 97 | 40 | 52 | 21 | 95 | 39 |

Note: Excludes double counting of disputes referred to more than one organization. Most successful organization is credited.

*Cases of "great" UN success in isolating disputes: Indonesian independence, status of Cyrenaica, KMT troops in Burma, Suez war, Zaire independence, status of African High Commission Territories, Yom Kippur war. Cases of "limited" UN success in isolating disputes: Corfu Channel, Greek civil war, Azerbaijan, Kashmir secession, Kashmir negotiations (1949-64), Korean negotiations (1951-53), British Cameroon, Lebanon/Jordan civil war (1958), Bizerta, Aden independence, Cyprus civil war, Panama Canal (1964), second Kashmir war and negotiations (1965-70), Six-Day war, Shatt-el-Arab, Cyprus invasion (1974), Cyprus negotiations, Belize independence, Western Sahara war, Benin coup, Litani River war.

percentage of such disputes not referred to any international organizations declined until 1970, hovered around one third of all such disputes during the 1970s, but rose to over half since 1980, while the UN's share declined to 32 percent—the lowest share in the history of the organization.* The regionals since 1980 also received the lowest share in their history of the global management load.

While these trends cast doubt on the continuing relevance of international collective security organizations, a look at Table 2 can be reassuring. Here the focus is on a subset of disputes that featured serious fighting, while Table 1 also included disputes in which only minor skirmishing and rioting took place. Serious disputes still go to international organizations. Only one third remained unreferred after 1980, the highest score since 1960. The UN's share of the load is over one half, up from the low point of 1971-75. The regionals, on the other hand, seem to be falling into disuse with respect to the management of serious conflict.

Unfortunately, not even this finding disposes of the issue of relevance. Table 3 contrasts the UN's experience as of 1980 with disputes referred to regional organizations and with nonreferred cases in terms of all the main variables relating to threats to the peace. Again we see that the UN does well because it is called on to manage the most serious cases of military threat. But the same is not true of other characteristics. The nonreferred cases include

Table 2

REFERRALS OF SERIOUS DISPUTES INVOLVING MILITARY OPERATIONS AND FIGHTING

| Era | Total Number | To United Nations | | To regionals | | Nonreferred | |
|---|---|---|---|---|---|---|---|
| | | Number | Percent | Number | Percent | Number | Percent |
| 1945-50 | 19 | 8 | 42% | -- | -- | 11 | 58% |
| 1951-55 | 5 | 3 | 60 | -- | -- | 2 | 40 |
| 1956-60 | 11 | 7 | 64 | -- | -- | 4 | 36 |
| 1961-65 | 23 | 10 | 44 | 7 | 30% | 6 | 26 |
| 1966-70 | 11 | 7 | 64 | 2 | 18 | 2 | 18 |
| 1971-75 | 12 | 4 | 33 | 5 | 42 | 3 | 25 |
| 1976-80 | 26 | 13 | 50 | 8 | 31 | 5 | 19 |
| 1981-84 | 15 | 8 | 53 | 2 | 13 | 5 | 33 |
| 1945-84 | 122 | 60 | 49 | 24 | 20 | 38 | 31 |

*Note:* Excludes double counting of disputes referred to more than one organization. Most successful organization is credited.

*This discussion is based on Table A in Appendix B below.

Table 3

ATTRIBUTES OF REFERRED AND NONREFERRED
DISPUTES AS OF 1980
*(In percent; N = 217)*

| Variable | Referred to UN | Referred to Regionals | Nonreferred |
|---|---|---|---|
| Intensity: High | 65% | 45% | 37% |
| Warfare: High | 30 | 24 | 14 |
| Spread: Regional/global | 23 | 38 | 22 |
| Issue: Cold war/decolonization | 55 | 20 | 61 |
| Parties: Cold war-aligned | 65 | 47 | 66 |
| Parties: Super/large | 46 | 18 | 45 |

*Source:* Haas (1983), Table A, p. 242.

more cold war and decolonization disputes, while the shares are about the same in terms of spread, alignment, and the relative power of the disputants. The UN cannot be said to be the preferred forum for the management of sharply defined types of disputes. It mirrors global context of strife quite accurately. What then explains its successes and failures?

## III

## CORRELATES OF UNITED NATIONS SUCCESS AND FAILURE

Let us examine first the forty-year record of the United Nations in terms of the overall statistical associations between success and the variables of salience, global context, and management. Specific features of certain cases and eras will be examined later.

The most intense disputes are the most likely to be successfully managed. Insignificant and very low intensity disputes can be marginally influenced. Disputes in the intermediate range are the most resistant to management.

Success comes most readily when the fighting is very limited. The most contagious disputes are the ones most frequently influenced, very often with great success. Disputes that the neighbors of the contending parties are about to enter actively are the most difficult to manage, whereas it seems relatively simple to score minimal impacts on purely bilateral disputes.

Disputes free of decolonization and cold war complications are the most successfully managed *provided* that no civil war is involved. On the other hand, such disputes arising out of an internal conflict are the most intractable. Decolonization issues are the next most amenable to UN management. Cold war disputes score lowest, although 37 percent of them were influenced by UN action.

Success is easier to achieve if the contending parties are members of the same cold war bloc or if both are nonaligned. Cold war alliances complicate conflict management.

Conflicts involving middle powers (such as Argentina, Mexico, Egypt, Pakistan, the Netherlands) are most easily managed, particularly when the opposing party is smaller. Conflicts involving a superpower as a party are the most intractable.

Strong UN decisions bring results. However, the failure to make a strong decision does not necessarily imply inability to influence the outcome of a dispute.

UN operations of a military nature are almost always successful. Field operations involving only the Secretariat are also successful over half the time. The failure to launch any operations results in failure of management two thirds of the time.

Successful action is associated most strongly with the joint leadership of the superpowers and the active intervention of the Secretary-General. But even the leadership of a single superpower brought success in 53 percent of the cases in which it occurred. When leadership is exercised by large and middle powers, the rate of success declines sharply. Small powers make the poorest leaders. Successful UN intervention requires a wide or very wide consensus of the membership.

There is an appreciable difference between situations of major impact and those in which a marginal impact was scored. Major impact is correlated with active warfare, decolonization issues (until 1965), disputes involving super and large powers (until 1970), strong decisions, large operations, and the leadership of the Secretary-General. These add up to a very restrictive profile of disputes on which the United Nations had a major impact. Much more versatility, however, is suggested by the cases in which we observe only minor impact. Instances of marginal effectiveness are spread over a wide spectrum of dispute attributes and modes of management. If the membership is sufficiently concerned, it appears the United Nations can still make a limited difference in a wide variety of circumstances even though the members will now tend not to use it in decisively abating, isolating, or settling their disputes.

The forty-year correlates of success and failure obscure wide fluctuations of impact from era to era. The UN started life with an impressive record of successful interventions. In the cold war years that followed, its impact declined, to be succeeded by its period of greatest effectiveness. In the early 1960s there was a decline of over 50 percent in its impact rate, but things got somewhat better in the late 1960s. In the decade of the 1970s success dropped to the lowest levels yet, followed by a still sharper drop after 1980. How account for these fluctuations?

## SALIENCE DOES NOT PREDICT SUCCESS

Until 1975 it could be said that success varied directly with the incidence of high intensity disputes (Figure 5). Since that time the association no longer holds; effectiveness diminished whether the percentage of severe disputes rose or fell. The decline in disputes with severe fighting after 1970 did not affect the impact of the UN; increases in such disputes after 1980 also had no effect. The incidence of disputes posing a danger of contagion has been about the same since 1970, seemingly without influencing the organization's performance. Clearly, trends in the salience of the cases referred to New York cannot explain the fluctuations unless other variables are considered at the same time. But we cannot escape the conclusion that states increasingly tolerate conflict rather than wish to manage it. No other inference seems possible if even reductions in the scope of fighting and bickering go together with declining overall success.

### GLOBAL CONTEXT PREDICTS BETTER

Does the shifting incidence of cold war and decolonization issues explain the fluctuations? Clearly, as the number of colonial situations requiring solution declines, the effectiveness of the UN suffers along with it (see Figure 6). Conversely, as the number of disputes unrelated to the meta-issues rises, the UN becomes less effective. Are disputes that pit members of cold war alignments and alliances against each other ineffectively managed, while disputes that feature states that are not cold war opponents are managed better, as Finlayson and Zacher suggest?* The evidence is not clearcut. Until 1970 disputes among the nonaligned and among members of the same alliance were indeed managed successfully more often. During the 1970s, a decade of increasing conflict among the smaller nonaligned states, the referrals of such disputes to the UN rose sharply, but impact dropped equally sharply. Yet after 1980— an era of renewed aggressive anti-Communist initiatives on the part of the United States—the relationship seems to hold again. It appears that marginality with respect to the major issues of global politics goes with an increasing reluctance of the membership to "get involved."

*See Jock A. Finlayson and Mark W. Zacher, "The United Nations and Collective Security," in *The United States, the United Nations, and the Management of Global Change*, ed. Toby Trister Gati (New York: New York University Press, 1983), pp. 162-83; and Mark W. Zacher, *International Conflicts and Collective Security, 1946-77* (New York: Praeger, 1979).

### CORRELATES OF SUCCESS AND FAILURE

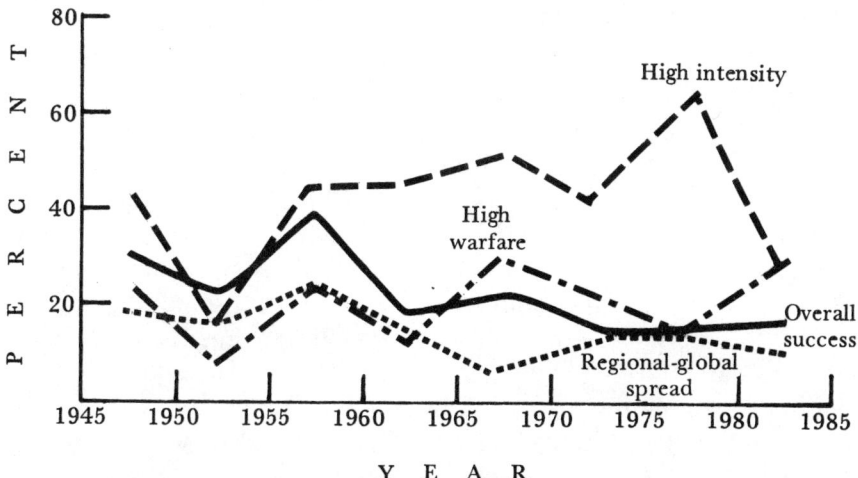

Figure 5. SALIENCE OF UNITED NATIONS DISPUTES
AND OVERALL SUCCESS *(N = 137)*

*Source:* Appendix B, Table B

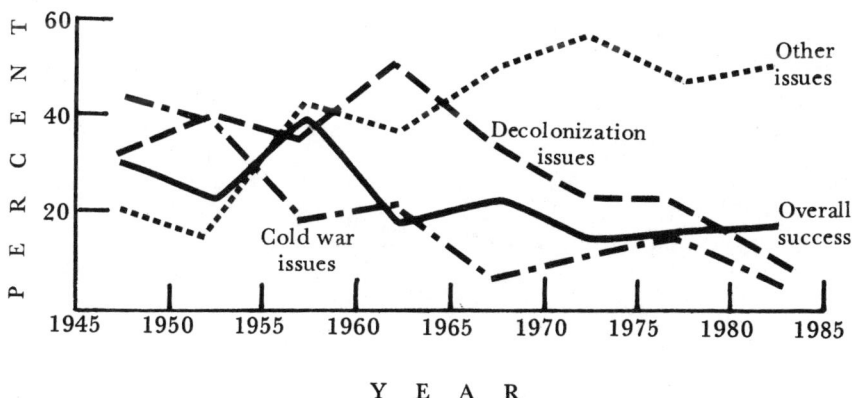

Figure 6. TYPES OF UNITED NATIONS DISPUTES
AND OVERALL SUCCESS *(N = 137)*

*Source:* Appendix B, Table B

## DISPUTES OVER RESOURCES: A NEW META-ISSUE?

What about the suggestion sometimes made that, with the waning of the cold war and the end of the decolonization process, a new deep-seated source of conflict has infected the global context? Those who make the suggestion consider the advent of disputes over economic resources to be of transcendent importance. I examined the 319 cases in the set to isolate territorial disputes that involved claims over agricultural land, mineral deposits, fishing rights, and access to rivers, lakes, and waterways. If the incidence of such disputes had increased over time, we would have reason to conclude that an economic resource meta-issue had emerged. No such pattern was found. Resource-related claims were inherent in many cold war, decolonization, and other disputes throughout the post-1945 period, but their incidence has not increased from decade to decade (see Table 4).

Table 4

### INCIDENCE OF RESOURCE-RELATED DISPUTES BY DECADES, 1945-1984

| | Referred to: | | | | | |
|---|---|---|---|---|---|---|
| | United Nations | | Regionals | | Nonreferred | |
| Decade | Number | Percent[a] | Number | Percent[a] | Number | Percent[a] |
| 1945-55 | 7 | 23% | 3 | 25% | 4 | 20% |
| 1956-65 | 10 | 24 | 7 | 23 | 2 | 8 |
| 1966-75 | 5 | 19 | 3 | 14 | 5 | 36 |
| 1976-84 | 8 | 22 | 7 | 30 | 8 | 22 |

[a]Percent of total disputes referred during the decade.

## ENERGETIC MANAGEMENT MAKES A DIFFERENCE

The explanation of the decline in UN effectiveness after 1970 lies in the growing indifference to conflict management of those most capable of action and leadership. The veto in the Security Council—of which we will have more to say—is not a key factor here because the General Assembly has been as reluctant as its oligarchic partner to mount major operations since 1970. The financial dispute over peacekeeping and truce observation missions is a symptom of this indifference, not its cause. If a sufficient number of member states were willing to shoulder the budgetary burdens voluntarily—as they did in the 1960s—the financial dispute would not prevent the mounting of major missions.

It is clear that strong decisions were associated with relatively effective management except for the 1975-80 era (Figure 7). During those five years successes were achieved only because of the large number of Secretariat missions charged with mediation, fact-finding, and monitoring.* It is not surprising that the growing failure rate since 1970 is associated with the decline in the willingness to mount military operations.

Successful interventions have to be led by somebody. The more powerful members of the United Nations have not taken a consistently prominent leadership role in conflict management since the early years of the organization (see Figure 8). It is clear that the leadership of the Secretary-General (which of course presupposes the support or at least the toleration of the major powers) is strongly associated with success. This association is pronounced in every era. The apparent lack of American leadership between 1955 and 1960 is misleading: that was the era of initiatives launched by Dag Hammarskjöld, usually with the active support of the United States. Since consensus has remained essentially the same since 1950, its independent influence on effectiveness is insignificant. Put the other way around, since the level of consensus on the management of disputes on the agenda has always been fairly stable and high, consensus is necessary for success but does not assure it.

SUMMARY

The number of variables influencing success is too large and the peculiarities of each era too great to permit a simple causal statement of what determines successful conflict management. We can only attempt a statement that captures the regular patterns observed for most eras, a minimal statement: Relatively successful conflict management is possible when a major power and/or the Secretary-General mobilize support for a strong resolution authorizing civilian

*During this period such missions were authorized in eleven disputes. No great impact was scored in any, but the only cases of outright failure were the Timor and Kampuchean disputes.

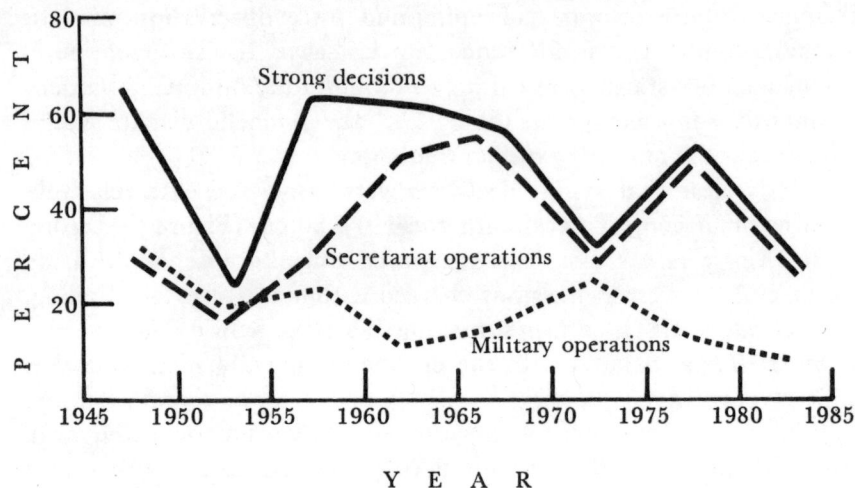

Figure 7. UNITED NATIONS: TYPES OF DECISIONS AND OPERATIONS *(N = 137)*

*Source:* Appendix B, Table D

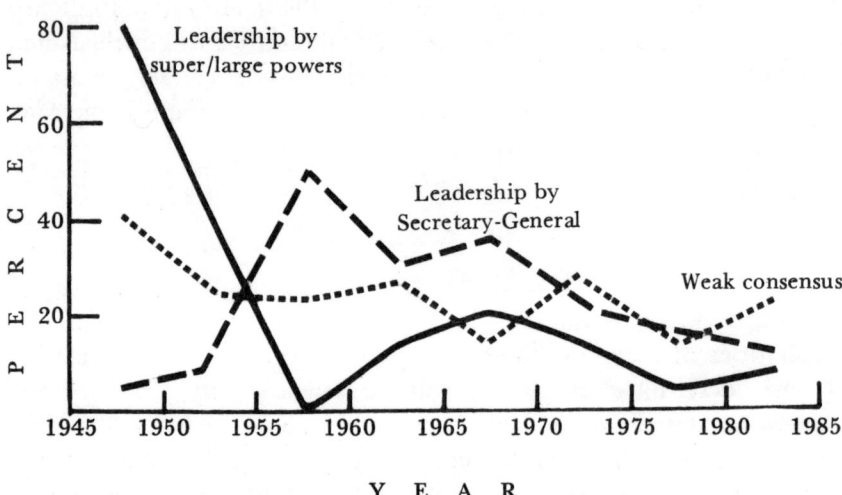

Figure 8. UNITED NATIONS: TYPES OF LEADERSHIP AND CONSENSUS *(N = 134)*

*Source:* Appendix B, Table D

or military field operations. This tends to take place only when the issue dividing the parties involves decolonization or a dispute which is *sui generis* and does not grow out of a civil war. No reliable associations that characterize each era with the salience of the dispute, the power of the contending parties, or consensus can be discovered.*

Is there a chance that the United Nations will continue to have at least a limited impact in some situations of conflict? For example, partly in response to UN involvement, in recent years the United States has moderated its power to act unilaterally in the Iranian hostage crisis and in the second Panama Canal episode. Similarly, because of UN involvement South Africa negotiated on Namibia, changed some apartheid rules, and reopened the border with Transkei. UN actions to postpone the lifting of sanctions against Rhodesia probably helped to topple the Smith government. The Secretary-General made some contribution to managing the Iranian hostage and Burmese refugee cases. Several of these disputes had spread beyond the immediate vicinity of conflict.

A true test of the possibility for continued relevance of the United Nations requires a systematic comparison of the core issues on the UN agenda. If it turns out that success is heavily concentrated on certain simple disputes involving the withdrawal of willing European countries from unwanted colonial possessions, or on Cyprus, or on the Middle East, then the argument for the United Nations' relevance is weak. Such a test is attempted in Table 5. "Easy decolonization" issues comprise cases about territories that the imperial power seemed eager to relinquish by the time the dispute reached the United Nations; "hard decolonization" disputes imply a strong reluctance on the part of the imperial power. The key test is the organization's pattern of success in managing "miscellaneous" issues. The United Nations seems to pass the test. Its success in the "miscellaneous" category after 1975 rose higher than it had been in its previously most successful era of 1956-60.

## DO REGIONAL ORGANIZATIONS UPSTAGE THE UN?

The regional record of success excels that of the United Nations in some of the contextual categories in which UN performance has been weak, but on the whole, with the exception of the period 1971-75,

*For further support of these conclusions, derived from analyzing the era-by-era correlates of great and limited success, see Appendix B, Tables E and F.

Table 5

UNITED NATIONS SUCCESS IN MANAGING POLITICAL ISSUES
*(In percent)*

|         | Number of Disputes | Decolonization | | Cold War[c] | Arab-Israel[d] | India-Pakistan[e] | Cyprus[f] | Miscellaneous[g] |
|---------|---|---|---|---|---|---|---|---|
| Period  |   | Easy[a] | Hard[b] | | | | | |
| 1945-50 | 13 | 15% | 23% | 32% | 15% | 15% | 0   | 0   |
| 1951-55 | 4  | 0   | 25  | 50  | 0   | 0   | 0   | 25% |
| 1956-60 | 12 | 8   | 42  | 8   | 8   | 0   | 0   | 34  |
| 1961-65 | 10 | 30  | 50  | 0   | 0   | 0   | 10% | 10  |
| 1966-70 | 9  | 33  | 11  | 0   | 22  | 11  | 0   | 22  |
| 1971-75 | 6  | 33  | 0   | 0   | 17  | 0   | 33  | 17  |
| 1976-80 | 16 | 12  | 12  | 12  | 19  | 0   | 0   | 44  |
| 1981-84 | 4  | 0   | 0   | 25  | 25  | 0   | 0   | 50  |

[a] Cyrenaica, Togoland, British Cameroon, African High Commission Territories, Kuwait, Panama Canal 1, Djibouti, Bahrein, Equatorial Guinea, Panama Canal 2, Transkei, New Hebrides, Belize

[b] Indonesia, French withdrawal from Levant, Namibia, West Irian, Algerian independence, Mauritania/Morocco, Sakiet raid, attack on Bizerta, Congo independence, Suez war, Aden independence, Ifni, Sarawak/Sabah, Rhodesian U.D.I., Falkland Islands, persecution in South Africa, raids into Angola

[c] Greek civil war, Azerbaijan, Korean negotiations, Russian wives, Corfu Channel, China Seas piracy, status of Laos, human rights in El Salvador, Afghanistan, Corinto mining

[d] Palestine independence, Palestine truce (1945-56), Israeli borders (1957-66), Six-Day war, Israeli borders (1967-73), Yom Kippur war, Litani River campaign, Israeli raids into Lebanon, Gaza/West Bank occupation, Baghdad reactor

[e] Kashmir secession, Kashmir negotiations, second Kashmir war

[f] Cyprus civil war, Turkish invasion of Cyprus, Cyprus negotiations

[g] KMT troops in Burma, Lebanon-Jordan civil wars, Wadi Halfa, Buraimi oasis, Thai-Cambodian border, Tutsi restoration attempt, Katanga exiles, Persian Gulf access, Chilean repression, U.S. hostages in Iran, Burmese refugees, coup in Benin, Farraka barrage, Western Sahara, Malta/Libya, Gulf war, Seychelles invasion, Essequibo

regional organizations dealt with cases that were far less intense than those the United Nations addressed. Given the membership of these organizations, the bulk of the disputes involved only the smallest states. Extra-regional states were often on the point of entering disputes in Africa and the Middle East, but this was not true in the western hemisphere. Civil strife accounted for 56 percent of the caseload. Less than 20 percent of the cases involved decolonization or the cold war, and only 30 percent pitted members of opposing cold war alliances against each other. Warfare was rarely involved.

Our purpose in examining the regional organizations' record in managing conflict is to test the hypothesis that regional organizations have a specialized capability for dealing with relatively localized, low-intensity disputes and thus complement the overall mandate of the United Nations. It is also hypothesized that the regionals are major competitors of the UN. "Forum shopping" is a well-known international sport, and states tend to appeal to the organization most likely to assure the success of the claim being advanced. For example, the United States appealed to the OAS for support in its interventions in the Dominican Republic and in Guatemala, while the Communist bloc appealed to the UN in the same cases. Both resulted in successes for the United States and the OAS and failures for the Communists and the UN. Repression in Chile was also taken up by both organizations; again the OAS was probably the more effective agent. Neither the UN nor the OAU found solutions to the Chad civil war or the Western Sahara conflict.

Prior to the Dominican Republic episode (1965), the Organization of American States was the most successful of all the collective security organizations, largely because the United States was able to use OAS procedures for giving multilateral legitimacy to unilateral moves in dealing with minor Caribbean and Central American disagreements. The advent of Soviet-aligned Cuba changed all that, along with the leftward drift of Latin American politics. The Dominican intervention was supported by a bare majority of the OAS membership. By the end of the 1970s, as in the Nicaraguan case, the United States was no longer able to marshal majorities for its preferred solutions, and the OAS went into decline. Cases previously handled by it now are routinely referred to the UN. Certainly the experience of the OAS since 1965 challenges the hypothesis that regional organizations complement the UN, although its record before 1965 provides considerable support for that view.

The record of the Arab League has undergone extreme fluctuations. It had a dismal record in its first decade, but performance improved during the 1960s and 1970s when there was increasing intensity of disputes, more active warfare, and greater threats of infection by regional and global confrontations. Apparently the success of the League during these decades is related to the desire of the member states to isolate the region from global (especially cold war-related) infection. Its early limited success in containing the Lebanese civil war and great success in stopping two wars between the Yemens support this interpretation. Success also seems to depend on strong Egyptian leadership. Since the Camp David agreements, there has been no strong leader, and no new disputes have been given to the League since 1979. A new Arab collective self-defense/collective security organization—the Gulf Cooperation Council—has emerged since that time, and has successfully managed two disputes (credited to the Arab League in our statistical summary). Thus the League has never been in rivalry with the UN, but during the 1960s and 1970s there was a limited complementarity between the two organizations.

The effectiveness of the OAU has oscillated more dramatically than that of the Arab League—from a success score of 22 percent in 1966-70 rising to 30 percent in 1971-75, only to slide back to 10 percent since 1976. During the 1970s its task became more difficult when African wars became more deadly, disputes spread more widely in and outside the region, and the disputing parties were increasingly aligned with one of the sides in the cold war. During 1966-75, half of the disputes grew out of civil wars and revolutions; during 1976-84 the number fell to six out of fourteen. Still, performance improved until the early 1970s, decisions became stronger, and one large operation was attempted in Chad. A look at the identity of the cases may suggest why.

During the 1960s the Secretary-General of the OAU sought an active role as conflict manager, a role strongly resisted by member states of more conservative views and opposed to Pan-Africanism. Succeeding secretaries-general have left the management role to heads of state. With leadership diffused, the fact that there is neither a strong executive head nor a hegemonic state (Nigeria's leadership has been intermittent) compels the OAU to seek American and French assistance whenever operations are contemplated. The OAU is incapable of mounting and financing operations on its own, and its success, when mediation by heads of state proves insufficient, depends on extra-regional actors. When these actors' goals in isolating African conflicts from the global context coincide with the OAU membership's, management action complementing that of the United Nations is possible.

Are regional organizations successful at UN expense? We would have to come to this conclusion if we found that the United Nations and the regionals are rivals for the same kinds of cases and if the regionals outperform the UN. Conversely, if we find that the typical profiles of disputes referred to the UN and the regionals are different, it would suggest a pattern of complementarity.

An examination of the twenty-two disputes submitted both to the United Nations and to one or more of the regionals allows one judgment of relative effectiveness (see Table 6).

Table 6

COMPARISON OF DISPUTES REFERRED TO
UN AND REGIONALS
(N = 22)

| Performance | Degree of Success in 1945-65 | | | Degree of Success in 1966-84 | | |
|---|---|---|---|---|---|---|
|  | None | Some | Great | None | Some | Great |
| Regionals do better | 0 | 3 | 2 | 0 | 1 | 2 |
| UN does better | 0 | 2 | 1 | 0 | 0 | 0 |
| No difference | 3 | 2 | 0 | 4 | 2 | 0 |

A study of other disputes that went only to the United Nations but match the profile of "typical" referrals to regional organizations permits another comparison. Typically disputes referred to a regional organization before 1965 involved minimal fighting, were of low intensity, and had not spread beyond the neighbors of the antagonists. Global meta-issues were seldom involved, the parties were small or middle powers, and they were either nonaligned or members of the same cold war bloc. If regionals consistently outperformed the United Nations in managing such conflicts, we would have to conclude that their specialized competence complemented that of the United Nations. The record suggests that this did not happen with any consistency, even though the OAS before 1965 performed in accordance with the ideal division of labor.

After 1965 the profile of disputes submitted to the regionals no longer differed systematically from the United Nations' caseload. The organizations became competitors for the same task, and the regionals outperformed the United Nations.

The same conclusion emerges from a second test. There were eight disputes referred to the United Nations that "normally" should have gone to the OAS and the Council of Europe, all after 1963; in four of these the United Nations scored successes, in a sense at the expense of regional organizations because the parties did not trust them. Hence we must conclude not only that the regionals are increasingly successful at UN expense but also that the reverse is true. There is no global division of labor among conflict management agencies now and there probably never was one.*

---

*This confirms Robert Butterworth's finding; see his "Organizing Collective Security: The UN Charter's Chapter VIII in Practice," *World Politics* 28 (January 1976): 197-222. Five of the eight cases involved aspects of confrontation between Greece and Turkey; the other three were Caribbean disputes to which the United States was a party. For additional evidence that states do not consistently coordinate policy in the United Nations with what is done in regional organizations, see Ernst B. Haas and Edward T. Rowe, "Regional Organizations in the United Nations: Is There Externalization?," *International Studies Quarterly* 17 (March 1973).

IV

## WHY MILITARY OPERATIONS ARE USUALLY SUCCESSFUL

United Nations military efforts most often cope with the proximate causes of conflict, not the underlying ones. They succeed in stopping or limiting hostilities; they isolate the combatants; they abate the conflict, but they do not settle it. Settlement came about in only four cases of a total of sixteen military missions. Nonmilitary interventions undertaken by the Secretary-General or his personal representative that engage in fact-finding, monitoring, and mediation are far more effective in resolving minor quarrels permanently. The UN is good at peacekeeping, but the membership has been averse to permit it to engage in peacemaking.

UN military tasks differ. Three broad categories are distinguishable, though all are loosely labelled as "peacekeeping." Military operations may take the form of enforcement measures designed to restrain an identified aggressor. This happened only during the Korean war. Nonmilitary enforcement measures, but including embargoes on military equipment, were authorized against Portugal, South Africa, and Rhodesia. Military enforcement also occurred during the Congo operation as an unplanned outgrowth of a peacekeeping mission.*

On six occasions military operations took the form of observer missions mandated to separate the parties, create buffer zones between them, mediate local cease-fires, and observe compliance with UN resolutions. On nine further occasions UN forces were given true peacekeeping responsibilities. In addition to the tasks observer missions carry out, these forces were asked to persuade one or both

---

*The complete breakdown of enforcement attempts looks like this: Voluntary measures imposing trade, diplomatic, and communications embargoes were authorized against Portugal in Africa (failed), against South African apartheid (failed), and against China/North Korea (inconclusive). Voluntary military sanctions were approved against China and North Korea (successful). Binding trade, diplomatic, and communications measures were imposed against Rhodesia (failed) and binding military measures against Katanga (successful).

sides to withdraw from forward positions (usually the party which was winning) and to interpose themselves in force between the combatants. In several of these cases the UN force was also given administrative responsibilities for dealing with civilians in the area. (The mandates of all UN military missions are summarized in Table 7.)

Only two military operations were outright failures. One scored only limited success. While moderate to great success was scored in the vast majority of cases, the differences in impact should be noted. In the cases of moderate success, UN forces failed to achieve some of the tasks they were given, or failed to carry out their missions successfully all of the time. For instance, UNTSO did not often succeed in preventing Arab raids into Israel and retaliatory Israeli operations. UNMOGIP failed to stop Pakistani infiltration into the Indian part of Kashmir in 1965, and then did not stabilize the front sufficiently to prevent the Indian attack in 1971. UNEF 1 did not stop the Egyptian moves in 1967. UNFICYP was unable to maintain the buffer zone in Cyprus against Turkish attacks in 1974, and has not yet succeeded in making the Turks withdraw their troops from the island. UNIFIL failed to keep the parties separated and proved incapable of stopping the Israeli invasion of Lebanon in 1982.

## SUCCESSFUL UN IMPACT MAY DEMAND ACTION OUTSIDE THE ORGANIZATION

It has become accepted UN practice in observer and peacekeeping operations *not* to identify any of the parties as aggressors. While UN impact on dispute settlement has been modest, one purpose of peacekeeping is the creation of conditions of stability and trust facilitating eventual settlement. This outcome cannot be achieved if the UN designates one of the parties as "guilty" before the negotiations get underway. This did not matter in the Korean case since the UN's mediatory role in arranging truce terms was confined to working out the modalities for dealing with prisoners of war. For purposes of demarcating and monitoring the truce lines, the "UN forces" remained a belligerent, not a peacekeeper. Nor did the problem arise in the Congo case, since the UN forces achieved a complete victory and the defeated party lacked sovereign status.

These cases of attempted enforcement suggest that action outside the UN framework is crucial to success. The voluntary embargoes against Portugal, South Africa, and China, because they were voluntary

## WHY MILITARY OPERATIONS ARE SUCCESSFUL

lacked consistent implementation. In the case of South Africa, even the declared champions of active anti-apartheid measures continue a *sub rosa* trade with Pretoria. The binding measures against Rhodesia were enforced, sometimes with British naval patrols off Mozambique, in order to prevent Portuguese aid to Salisbury. However, these measures seemed to stiffen the determination of the Smith government to resist.

Why does peacekeeping so rarely contribute to the permanent settlement of a conflict? How does it relate to extra-UN measures on the part of the members? Permanent settlement did come about in Indonesia (UNCI), Zaire (ONUC), and Sinai after 1973 (UNEF 2). In each case the United States, through unilateral means, put pressure on the stronger party to give way. In the case of West Irian (UNTEA), such pressure was not necessary since there was little interest in the Netherlands for retaining the territory. The success of UNEF 2, ONUC, UNTEA, and UNCI, in other words, was made possible by the existence of a *prior agreement* among the main parties on how the dispute was to be resolved. The agreement was reached outside the UN. Peacekeeping was necessary for consummating the agreement, not for making it. It is therefore a tribute to the effectiveness of the UN that even in the absence of prior agreement on a permanent settlement, successful impacts could be scored in eight major disputes.*

The question of extra-UN pressure can be approached in another way. Is the success of a military operation dependent on a prior agreement by the party which appears to be winning to halt its advance and withdraw from advanced positions? The relevant information (taken from Table 8) is as follows:

| *Appeared to be winning* | *Agreed to withdraw* |
|---|---|
| Communist forces in Greece | No |
| Dutch forces in Indonesia | Yes |
| Israeli forces in Sinai (1956) | Yes |
| U.S. forces in Lebanon (1958) | Yes |
| Belgian forces in Zaire | Yes |

*In ten of the other twelve cases of military operations there were no such prior agreements. UNEF 1 was put in place in the context of negotiations resulting in the withdrawal of British, French, and Israeli forces, again due to pressure by the United States. UNOGIL was mounted with an understanding that U.S. forces withdraw from Lebanon. Prior agreements thus did help to assure UN success even though no permanent settlement resulted.

Table 7

MANDATES OF UNITED NATIONS MILITARY OPERATIONS

| Operation | Authorized by | Make one side withdraw | Separate parties | Create buffer | Mediate truce | Observe compliance with UN resolution | Civilian administration tasks | Overall Impact |
|---|---|---|---|---|---|---|---|---|
| UNSCOB 1946-49 [Greece] | General Assembly | | | | | X | | Moderate |
| UNCI 1947-48 [Indonesia] | Security Council | X | X | | X | X | | Great |
| UNTSO 1948-56 [Palestine] | SC | | X[a] | | X | X | | Moderate |
| UNMOGIP 1948- [Kashmir] | SC | | X[a] | X | X | X | | Great |
| Korea Truce[b] 1951-53 | GA | | | | X | | | Great |
| UNEF 1 1956-67 [Sinai] | GA | X | X[a] | X | X | X | X | Great |
| UNOGIL 1958 [Lebanon] | SC | X | | | | X | | Moderate |
| ONUC[b] 1960-64 [Zaire] | GA | X | X | | X | X | X | Great |

WHY MILITARY OPERATIONS ARE SUCCESSFUL   39

Table 7 (continued)

| Operation | Authority | | | | | | | Success |
|---|---|---|---|---|---|---|---|---|
| UNTEA 1962-63 [West Irian] | GA | X | | | | X | X | Great |
| UNYOM 1963-64 [Yemen] | SC | | $X^a$ | $X^a$ | $X^a$ | $X^a$ | | None |
| UNFICYP 1964-73 [Cyprus] | SC | | $X^a$ | $X^a$ | X | X | X | Moderate |
| 1974- | | $X^a$ | X | X | X | X | X | Moderate |
| UNIPOM 1965-66 [India-Pakistan] | SC | X | X | X | X | X | | Great |
| UNEF 2 1973-79 [Sinai] | SC | X | X | X | X | X | | Great |
| UNDOF 1974- [Syria] | SC | X | X | X | X | X | | Great |
| UNIFIL 1978- [Lebanon] | SC | X | $X^a$ | $X^a$ | $X^a$ | X | X | Some |
| UNTAG 1978- [Namibia] | SC | $X^a$ | $X^a$ | | X | $X^a$ | $X^a$ | None |

*Source:* Henry Wiseman, ed., *Peacekeeping* (New York: Pergamon, 1983).

[a] Task not successfully carried out.
[b] Task evolved in context of enforcement measures.

Table 8

## CONTEXT OF UNITED NATIONS MILITARY OPERATIONS

| Operation | Overall Impact | Directed against one party? | Did stronger party accept withdrawal before operation? | Did the parties agree on: | | |
|---|---|---|---|---|---|---|
| | | | | Mandate? | Duration? | Composition? |
| UNSCOB 1946-49 | Moderate | Yes | No | No[a] | No[a] | No[a] |
| UNCI 1947-48 | Great | Yes | Yes | Yes | No[a] | No[a] |
| UNTSO 1948-56 | Moderate | No | n.a. | No[a] | No[b] | No[b] |
| UNMOGIP 1948- | Great | No | n.a. | Yes | Yes | Yes |
| Korea Truce 1951-53 | Great | Yes | n.a. | Yes | Yes | Yes |
| UNEF 1 1956-67 | Great | Yes | Yes | Yes | No[b] | Yes |
| UNOGIL 1958 | Moderate | Yes | Yes | Yes | No[b] | No[b] |
| ONUC 1960-64 | Great | Yes | Yes | No[a] | No[b] | No[b] |

Table 8 (continued)

| | | | | | |
|---|---|---|---|---|---|
| UNTEA 1962-63 | Great | Yes | Yes | Yes | Yes |
| UNYOM 1963-64 | None | No | n.a. | Yes | No$^b$ |
| UNFICYP 1964-73 1974- | Moderate Moderate | No Yes | n.a. No | Yes No$^a$ | Yes Yes | Yes No$^b$ |
| UNIPOM 1965-66 | Moderate | No | n.a. | No$^a$ | No | No$^b$ |
| UNEF 2 1973-79 | Great | Yes | Yes | Yes | Yes | No$^b$ |
| UNDOF 1974 | Great | No | Yes | Yes | Yes | Yes |
| UNIFIL 1978- | Some | Yes | No | Yes | Yes | No$^b$ |
| UNTAG 1978- | None | Yes | No | No$^a$ | No$^a$ | No$^a$ |

$^a$Terms imposed by General Assembly or Security Council.

$^b$Terms worked out by Secretary-General without seeking consent of parties.

| | |
|---|---|
| Dutch forces in West Irian | Yes |
| Turkish forces in Cyprus (1974) | No |
| Israeli forces in Suez (1973) | Yes |
| Israeli forces in Syria (1973) | Yes |
| Israeli forces in Lebanon (1978, 1982) | Yes |
| South African forces in Namibia | No |

Clearly, in the large majority of cases, the consent of the stronger side seems to be a prerequisite for the UN's success. Obtaining that consent usually depends on the diplomatic and even military pressure of a superpower.

There is a connection between leadership, political alignment, and the type of issue in determining when and whether such pressure on behalf of UN operations will be exercised. I turn next to the exploration of that connection.

MUST THE UN BE "NEUTRAL" TO SUCCEED?

The fact that members of the UN very rarely stigmatize one of their number as an "aggressor" does not guarantee that even-handed neutrality characterizes UN military operations. UN military operations can and often do favor one side in a dispute. As Israelis never tire to point out, UN intervention for them means being robbed of a victory over their Arab antagonists (see listing above). Of the sixteen military episodes (seventeen, if we consider UNFICYP to include two different situations), ten were clearly directed against one party, thus favoring the other. Yet nine of these ten were cases of UN success. Neutrality is not a required ingredient. The conventional wisdom holds that peacekeeping ought to be successful in situations in which universal norms are being upheld at the expense of the particularistic norms of blocs or alliances. Neutrality should assure success, and the improvement of peacekeeping should depend on the implementation of universal norms.* Why is the conventional wisdom wrong?

Neutrality is not required for success when (1) the action corresponds to the preferences of the permanent members of the Security Council—i.e., the conditions of the concert are met, (2) one superpower leads and enjoys a two-thirds majority in the General Assembly even though other major powers may oppose, (3) the

---

*This is the argument made by Henry Wiseman in *Peacekeeping* (New York: Pergamon, 1983), pp. 365-67.

Secretary-General is able to construct temporary and shifting coalitions backing an intervention either in the Security Council or the General Assembly. (This condition also requires the support of one superpower.) Alternative routinized procedures that prevailed during specific periods in the history of the UN illustrate these conditions in action.

If we isolate certain features of UN practice, the historical record breaks down into four eras, though they overlap a bit. The features of interest are (1) the overall pattern of polarity in world politics, (2) the salience of the cold war in world politics and the alignments among states that show up in UN behavior as a result, (3) the leadership exercised by the cold war superpowers in the United Nations, and (4) the consensus among the other members they are to mobilize. The combination of these four features gives us periods I label "the concert" (1945-47 and occasionally thereafter), "permissive enforcement with balancing" (1948-55), "permissive engagement" (1956-70), and—despite my best efforts to find a pattern—a rather chaotic period of "no pattern" at all since 1970. The initial period of "the concert" corresponds to the UN Charter, which I have described earlier.

The importance of changes in procedures is demonstrated by the frequency and impact of the veto in the Security Council (see Table 9). The veto has a much more ambiguous relationship to the practice of collective security than is usually supposed. The United States did not have to use its veto before 1966 whereas the earlier frequent Soviet use, though it was not nearly as frequent as folklore maintains, ebbed at that point. The United States and its major allies had regular recourse to the veto after 1966, while the Soviets were able to do without it until the most recent reemergence of the cold war. At no time, however, has the veto crippled the United Nations. Changes in procedures made possible continued impact on conflict management despite recourse to the veto.*

---

*Data for the top part of Table 9 came from Robert S. Junn, "Voting in the United Nations Security Council," *International Interactions* 9, 4 (1983). I thank Professor Junn and the editors of *International Interactions* for permission to use the data. The French and British vetoes primarily sheltered South Africa and Rhodesia during the 1970s, though they also blocked the U.S.-sponsored resolution against Israel in 1956. American vetoes blocked sanctions against South Africa in 1976 and 1980 and also sheltered Rhodesia and Israel against condemnations. Recent U.S. vetoes relate to the Nicaraguan and Grenada conflicts. Soviet vetoes were often cast to oppose resolutions

Table 9

THE VETO AND UN SUCCESS

| Era | Number | Vetoes Cast on Disputes in Data Set[a] | | | | |
|---|---|---|---|---|---|---|
| | | USSR | US | UK | France | China |
| 1945-50 | 8 | 6 | 0 | 1 | 1 | 0 |
| 1951-55 | 3 | 3 | 0 | 0 | 0 | 0 |
| 1956-60 | 7 | 5 | 0 | 1 | 1 | 0 |
| 1961-65 | 5 | 4 | 0 | 1 | 0 | 0 |
| 1966-70 | 3 | 2 | 1 | 0 | 0 | 0 |
| 1971-75 | 9 | 0 | 5 | 2 | 1 | 1 |
| 1976-80 | 11 | 4 | 2 | 2 | 3 | 0 |
| 1981-84 | 5 | 1 | 4 | 0 | 0 | 0 |
| Totals | 51 | 26 | 12 | 7 | 6 | 1 |

| Era | Number | UN Impact Despite Veto | | | Percent |
|---|---|---|---|---|---|
| | | None | Some | Great | |
| 1945-50 | 8 | 2 | 2 | 4 | 75% |
| 1951-55 | 3 | 2 | 1 | 0 | 33 |
| 1956-60 | 7 | 1 | 0 | 6 | 86 |
| 1961-65 | 5 | 3 | 2 | 0 | 40 |
| 1966-70 | 3 | 2 | 0 | 1 | 33 |
| 1971-75 | 9 | 5 | 3 | 1 | 44 |
| 1976-80 | 11 | 7 | 4 | 0 | 36 |
| 1981-84 | 5 | 4 | 1 | 0 | 20 |
| Totals | 51 | 26 | 13 | 12 | 49 |

[a] The actual number of vetoes cast on issues relating to conflict management was 100, 59 of which were cast by the USSR and 21 by the United States. The difference in numbers is accounted for by the fact that more than one veto was cast on most of the disputes in the set, whereas I counted only one veto per case per state. However, I counted multiple vetoes in a given dispute as separate votes—e.g., when both France and Britain voted against the Suez peacekeeping force.

that dealt with decolonization cases, demonstrating Soviet dissatisfaction with measures considered too weak. On many other occasions Soviet vetoes merely blocked Western-inspired propaganda statements and therefore lacked substantive impact.

*The concert.* The initial period was one of the United Nations' most successful. The fact that cold war alignments did not interfere with its impact in Indonesia, the Levant, Azerbaijan, and Palestine is partly accounted for by the Soviet Union's not insisting on all the ground rules of the concert and accepting the strong leadership of the United States. The Soviet Union's restraint enabled the concert to function, a condition no doubt helped by a partial convergence of its interests with America's.

*Permissive enforcement with balancing.* The Greek civil war and the Korean war spelled the end of the concert; they implied the advent of tight bipolarity and full cold war alignments inside and outside the United Nations, and the United States commanded a two-thirds majority by virtue of the alignments. "Mutual abstention" in the use of the United Nations by the superpowers gave way to its employment for cold war purposes. The membership applications of states suspected of joining either alignment were blocked. The Soviet Union considered the Secretary-General a lackey of the West. After the predictable Soviet response to American dominance — the use of the veto in crises such as the Greek and Korean wars — the United States used its overwhelming majority to initiate the "Uniting for Peace" procedures by shifting collective security operations from the Security Council to the General Assembly. While the impact of the United Nations on conflict management declined after 1950, it remained a respectable 24 percent.

The authorization of enforcement measures by the General Assembly remained "permissive" because it carried no binding force; a vote merely authorized states willing to undertake an operation to do so. The Assembly legitimizes a decision by a state or an alliance, making the United Nations an adjunct of the alliance — or so it would be if the norm were permitted to work unchecked. The Korean war and its eventual settlement, however, suggest that permissive enforcement dominates only as long as the two-thirds majority of the sponsoring states remains unimpaired. If some states change their minds and decide to attempt mediation or conciliation between the antagonists, permissive enforcement yields to "balancing." Obviously the antagonists would not consent to balancing unless they had decided on their own that a continuation of the conflict was undesirable. During the period 1948-55, then, this combination of circumstances prevented the United Nations from becoming simply an appendage of one superpower, like the OAS.

*Permissive engagement.* The changes initiated during the late 1940s and the early 1950s were expanded and routinized between 1956 and 1965, a period that saw some of the United Nations' more dramatic successes and included a success score of 40 percent in 1956-60. Tight bipolarity gave way to a much looser constellation of forces as the Non-aligned Movement was organized and as the large number of newly independent states joined neither alliance, acquiring after 1960 a two-thirds majority in the United Nations. At the same time the internal cohesion of both cold war alliances declined and, for reasons unrelated to the United Nations, the salience of the cold war ebbed, resulting in the first detente after the Cuban missile crisis. The dissolution of colonial empires was at the top of the international conflict agenda and dominated the UN caseload, though this trend interacted with cold war considerations in some instances. Furthermore, this context provided the opportunity for Dag Hammarskjöld's "quiet diplomacy"—the engagement of the United Nations under "Uniting for Peace" auspices but no longer under the exclusive aegis of the United States and the West. The enlarged membership gave the Secretary-General the opportunity to base UN intervention on shifting coalitions of supporting states, often including the United States as an enthusiastic backer. The Soviets, while sometimes on the losing end of these coalitions, nevertheless reduced their use of the veto.

These adjustments, however, were bought at a price. The Charter stipulations governing membership eligibility were forgotten. So was the prohibition on interventions impinging on domestic jurisdiction. Hammarskjöld's invention of peacekeeping carried with it dependence on the General Assembly and resulted in the abandonment of the distinctions embodied in chapters 6 and 7 of the Charter. This in turn eventuated in the serious controversy over the independent powers of the Secretary-General, and the obligatory financing of peacekeeping operations not authorized by the Security Council. Not even an advisory opinion of the International Court of Justice disposed of the matter, even though it legitimated the routines initiated by Hammarskjöld. The powers assumed by the Secretary-General in requesting, recruiting, organizing, deploying, and supplying peacekeeping forces remained controversial. Yet the principle of earmarked standby military forces had become a victim of the "Uniting for Peace" procedure and of the ad hoc peacekeeping mechanism, and that mechanism became unreliable because of the dispute over financing. Because the active involvement of the General Assembly depended on the existence of an appropriate and stable coalition, predictable and consistent adherence to the new conflict management routines could not be attained, though occasional successes could. The nature of the issue and of the alliance commitment of the membership determined whether peacekeeping would occur.

*The current era.* No fundamental change occurred after 1970. Institutional innovations made earlier continued to be used, even though no peacekeeping operation was authorized by the General Assembly since 1963. The Security Council, however, continued to be sidestepped in other conflict management attempts to restrain Israel, South Africa, and Rhodesia. Peacekeeping, or any form of strong conflict management, was not used when Indonesia conquered Timor, China attacked Vietnam, Vietnam invaded Kampuchea, Iraq moved into Iran, and India aided secessionist Bangladesh, and no strong efforts were made to prevent several Middle Eastern countries from fueling the civil wars in Eritrea and Chad. Appeals by regional organizations to the UN to intervene in Kampuchea, Chad, Western Sahara, and the Iran-Iraq war went unheeded.\*
A double standard seemed to prevail in conflict management as the membership was less inclined to intervene energetically in conflicts among third world nations, even though it continued to make use of earlier institutional innovations as they had evolved in decolonization cases and in disputes involving Israel and South Africa.

One explanation lies in the changing nature of alignments and consensus, which in turn represents a major shift in the international environment. During the period before 1965, the nonaligned states were fewer in number and less united on issues. They became numerically dominant after 1965 as some Latin American and African states previously aligned with the United States joined them. The Non-Aligned Movement as a whole gained cohesion from its program for a New Interational Economic Order. (The fact that most nonaligned states also depend for favors on their oil-rich colleagues is not irrelevant.) Another reason lies in the decline of meta-issues: the cold war and decolonization gave way to disputes that involved issues specific to the antagonists in a given conflict. The additional fact that superpower leadership was muted goes hand in hand with the decline of polarity—the disintegration of the loose bipolar clusters into a congeries of unstable blocs that must tolerate crossovers among their members on a case-to-case basis.

\*Such requests were made by ASEAN, OAU, and the Islamic Conference.

While many of these conditions were also visible during the relatively successful years between 1966 and 1970, leadership, consensus, and alignment mark the difference from the current period. The 1966-70 period saw the advent of issues other than the cold war and decolonization, the emergence of middle and small powers as the main contestants, and a rise in the intensity of warfare, especially in local and bilateral disputes—all characteristic as well of the period since 1970. On the other hand, leadership by the Secretary-General was still significant then, one or both of the contestants in disputes was still a member of a cold war coalition 71 percent of the time, and consensus was at its highest point in UN history. Hence there was still room for permissive engagement. There may still be now, but the overt commitment of the member states gives little evidence of the necessary interest. Conflict management behavior, then, mirrors the fact that the nonaligned majority can agree on collective action when a dispute triggers the issue of racism or Zionism, but the nonaligned cannot be expected to be similarly united when wars among their own members are at issue. The permanent members of the Security Council take sides or urge action only when their own interests are involved—as in the Middle East and Cyprus. The result is a United Nations whose members are fundamentally divided on the importance of conflict management as a task.

### WHY AD HOC PROCEDURES SUFFICE FOR SUCCESSFUL PEACEKEEPING

When conditions relating to leadership, consensus, alignment, and issue salience are right, successful peacekeeping can take place even if the procedures for organizing, staffing, and paying for the operation remain fluid. We know that the controversy over these questions has been on the UN's agenda since 1963 and that no institutional formula has found acceptance. Why does the absence of agreement make little difference?

Thirty-three states contributed personnel to observer missions, while forty-seven states made military forces available for peacekeeping operations. Each operation had to be organized from scratch, a task made manageable by the fact that the Secretariat was able to "cannibalize" existing forces in UNFICYP and UNTSO to staff additional operations in the same general area, though the depleted forces then required reinforcements which had to be recruited anew. These figures, however, obscure the real truth: peacekeeping has been made possible by the willingness of a very small number of states to make their forces available almost all of the time. These are (with the number of operations served in parentheses) Canada (12), Sweden (10), Norway (9), Italy (9), Denmark (8), Finland (8), United States (8), Australia (7), Netherlands (6), Ireland (5), New Zealand (5), India (5). It is often said that such operations demand the *absence* of the superpowers, yet the United States shows up as a prominent participant. American participation took the form of logistic and transportation services rather than military personnel on the ground. However, without these services, several of the most successful peacekeeping operations could not have been mounted. British forces participated four times, and France did once. Soviet officers served as observers and Warsaw Pact troops took part in UNEF 2. Under conditions approximating the concert, there is no reason why such forces should not be used.

Improvisation suffices because the regular contributors have taken steps to train personnel in peacekeeping duties at the national and—in Scandinavia—the regional level. They have designated certain standby units though the UN has agreed neither on such forces nor on the training and logistic services essential for their success. ONUC and UNEF 1 could not have been successful without disproportionate Indian support; UNFICYP depended on heavy British contributions; UNEF 2 might have failed had the United States not assumed responsibility for the electronic monitoring of military movements in the Sinai. The semi-official International Peace Academy has undertaken the burden of systematic international training in the absence of the UN's ability to do so. However, it remains true that even improvisation would not have done the job unless the UN Secretariat had become the institutional memory for peacekeeping operations, making possible the creation of new forces on the basis of routines found to have been successful in earlier ones. (I shall return to this point.)

Finance remains a more serious obstacle to successful peacekeeping. Improvisation has so far done the job. True, the long labors of the General Assembly's Committee of 33 have not resulted in a consensual formula for regularizing the mode of financing these operations, nor have they disposed of the related matter of defining the powers of the Secretariat. The United States continues to demand the full implementation of the ICJ decision while the Soviets persist in their principled objection to it. France has moderated its initial opposition to obligatory financing.

Politically speaking, however, these legal positions have not prevented the mounting of peacekeeping operations when a sufficient consensus was in evidence—a situation approximating the condition of the concert. It is also true that lacking such a consensus the division on the basic principle impairs the ability of the UN to make use of the "Uniting for Peace" procedure. But permissive engagement remains possible if and when one of the superpowers is willing to swallow its principles and make the necessary voluntary contribution to fund an operation blocked in the Security Council. Despite its determination not to contribute more than 25 percent of the total UN budget, the United States financed 37 percent of UNEF 1 every year. Its contributions to UNFICYP hovered around 40 percent per year until 1971, and they rose to 50 percent for the period 1973-78. On the other hand, the expenses for the three UN forces separating Israel from the Arabs since 1974 have been largely borne by the regular UN budget, a signal victory for the American position and an indication that the Soviet Union will not act on principle when its local interests are actively engaged. While these operations were authorized by the Security Council, consonant with the Soviet position, the independent powers exercised by the Secretariat remained in excess of Soviet preferences, and the Soviet Union vetoed the continuation of UNEF 2. A clarification of the legal issue would obviously make possible more predictable UN operations.

## HOW VITAL IS THE LEADERSHIP OF THE SECRETARY-GENERAL?

But such a clarification is not likely to come about soon. What is at stake in the financial dispute is the question of *who* takes the initiative in requesting a military intervention and managing it—the Secretary-General, the Security Council (read the permanent members), or the General Assembly. Conventionalized routines developed since 1970 resulted in the current uneasy formula of permitting the Secretary-General to manage such operations, while reaffirming the power of the Security Council to authorize them and to define their mandates. During the 1970s the General Assembly became the loser, even though the West European countries as recently as 1978 pressed for a reaffirmation of its role in peacekeeping. Similarly, it was the

West Europeans, as the most active and committed peacekeepers, who unsuccessfully pressed for a codification of the Secretariat's powers in the Committee of 33.

When the Soviet Union in 1958 began its campaign to make the operations of the Secretariat subject to close control by the superpowers, the Secretary-General found various ways of protecting his independence despite the adoption of a troika-like formula for staffing the top posts in the Secretariat. The successful circumvention of the Soviet efforts had then the full support of the United States. This situation changed in the early 1970s. Despite their espousal of opposing views in the Committee of 33, the superpowers apparently came to an agreement on how peacekeeping ought to be mounted. The General Assembly, volatile and not easily controlled, was to be cut out altogether. The Security Council would again have sole responsibility for authorizing military operations. But the exact powers of the Secretary-General remain ambiguous, even though the United States remains in principle supportive of his strong role. The manner in which the Security Council can delegate responsibility over peacekeeping is still the main unresolved issue.

A look at the record makes clear that the role of the Secretary-General and of the Secretariat has been absolutely crucial in the exercise of successful peacekeeping (see Table 8). Trygve Lie worked out the terms under which UNTSO operates; Dag Hammarskjöld designed most of the terms for UNEF 1, UNOGIL, and ONUC; U Thant did likewise for UNYOM and UNIPOM; Kurt Waldheim carried out somewhat similar tasks for UNEF 2 and UNIFIL. In the remaining operations, in which the parties themselves agreed on mandate, duration, and composition of the forces, it was the Secretariat which assumed almost full responsibility for recruiting, deploying, and supplying the troops. Neither the Security Council nor the General Assembly was able to exercise operational control on a daily basis. It was the job of the Secretary-General to negotiate the status-of-forces agreements which defined the terms of access. Hence the future of the Secretariat's role is of some importance in the continued practice of peacekeeping.

## WHAT REFORMS ARE CONCEIVABLE?

The manner in which UNEF 2 was organized is a possible indicator of a future division of labor between the Security Council and the Secretariat. The Secretary-General's ability to recruit national contingents was circumscribed by the Soviet insistence on equitable geographical distribution. His appointment of a commander had to be approved by the Council, and even though the commander reported to the Secretary-General, frequent Secretariat reporting to the Security Council was mandatory, including all matters affecting "the nature of continued effective functioning of the Force." Costs were borne as general expenses of the organization, subject to the Soviet warning that this formula can be used only as long as the Security Council continues to exercise its supervision. France agreed with this proviso, while China refused to contribute. Duration was fixed for six months, with renewal requiring Security Council consent. In 1978, because of its challenge to the Camp David agreement, the Soviet Union withheld its consent for a further extension of the force's mandate. The concert came to an end, and with it routinized peacekeeping based on a symbiotic relationship between the Council and the Secretariat.

Must this situation continue? Critics of the ad hoc nature of peacekeeping have made a number of suggestions for improvements that accept the primacy of the Security Council as inescapable, and perhaps even desirable. Most of these proposals hinge on a revival of the dormant Military Staff Committee, or an analogous Security Council Committee to be set up. The proposals submitted to the Committee of 33 by Britain and Canada exemplify this approach.* The Military Staff Committee (or a new committee) would be composed of the permanent members as well as the states who contribute most frequently to peacekeeping. The Secretariat would become a consultant and adviser to the committee. The Security Council would have sole responsibility for authorizing a force, defining its mandate and duration, arranging for financial support, and redefining the force mission. The Secretary-General would have the power to determine the size and composition of the force, appoint the commander, conclude agreements with contributing states and the host countries, and instruct the commander on specific operations. A Council member has the right to challenge any decision of the Secretary-General, and action must be suspended until the challenge is voted on. Big power unanimity is reaffirmed. A host country has the right to challenge the composition of the force. These proposals go a long way toward limiting the kinds of initiatives Secretaries-General have been able to take in the past.

*UN documents, A/SPC/152 and A/9144, 9 October 1972 and 6 September 1973.

More ambitious proposals are also available. One refers to the situation in 1967 in which war was unleashed by the Secretary-General's decision to honor Egypt's request that UNEF 1 be withdrawn, in recognition of the principle that the consent of the host state is essential. The proposal would create a rule that any withdrawal of forces must be preceded by the approval of the Security Council or the General Assembly. It has been suggested that peacekeeping become a new human right.* The consent requirement would be eliminated in situations of civil war; the Secretary-General would have the power to intervene without the right of the political organs to block action, provided the main task is the establishment of order and the protection of basic human rights *without* the UN's taking any position, or aiding any one party in a civil war, with respect to the political issues at stake. Strict neutrality with respect to the question of right and justice would have to be observed. In view of our findings on the salience of alignments and issues in the practice of peacekeeping, this suggestion would seem far from the mark.

Less ambitious proposals also abound. They relate mostly to the earmarking and training of peacekeeping forces before the need for their deployment arises. An early-warning system to alert the UN to situations likely to require intervention has been proposed. It seems that a perusal of the daily newspaper would suffice for this job. Formal standby and training agreements are proposed. It appears as if the ad hoc arrangements now prevailing can do the job. A special United Nations Preparedness Review Group was suggested some years ago. The Committee of 33 has failed to endorse it, though the idea would make official what the International Peace Academy and the Scandinavian and Canadian governments do already.

None of these ideas seems timely, given the growing indifference to local wars on the part of many UN members and the continuing effectiveness of peacekeeping, ad hoc though it is, under conditions when a consensus for action does exist. Things could certainly be a lot worse.

---

*K. Venkata Raman, "United Nations Peacekeeping and the Future of World Order," in Wiseman.

## V

## COULD THINGS BE BETTER?

Misunderstanding of our problem and discouragement with the results so far achieved may . . . be attributed, in no small degree, to a lack of historical perspective in surveying the world as we find it today. . . . The United Nations is no stronger than the collective will of the nations that support it. Of itself it can do nothing. It is a machinery through which the nations can cooperate. It can be used and developed. . . or it can be discarded and broken.*

The words were written by Trygve Lie in 1946. They remain fully accurate in 1986.

No doubt things could be better, but not unless nation-states cease being themselves. Yet selfhood is dynamic. Governments today do not behave as their predecessors did in 1786 or 1886 or even in 1936. The UN has not gone the way of the League of Nations. The collective management of conflict remains on the agenda of international politics and continues to moderate disputes, albeit less effectively than twenty years ago. Management is not monopolized by the big powers, as it was in the nineteenth and early twentieth centuries; the participation of smaller states is itself an evolutionary step in the direction of a new selfhood. We must remind ourselves that at this moment five UN military operations are underway, made possible in large measure by the willingness of small countries to contribute to conflict management.

I now turn to the question of how much worse or how much better international conflict management could be if the UN had not existed, or if a different kind of international organization were to arise. This effort, first of all, calls for an answer to the questions raised in the beginning of this essay.

---

*Andrew W. Cordier and Wilder Foote, eds., *The Public Papers of the Secretaries-General of the United Nations*, vol. I (New York: Columbia University Press, 1969), p. 55.

## UNITED NATIONS IMPACT ON WORLD POLITICS

The impact of the UN on moderating international conflict has been marginal, but not absent. Abatement of disputes without settling or isolating them is the UN's major contribution. Its ability to stop hostilities is confined to Arab-Israeli and Cypriot confrontations and to certain cases of decolonization.

There is a trend toward conflict management that avoids referral to international organizations, though the most severe disputes continue to appear on the UN agenda.

Meta-issues are less important now than earlier. Resource-related issues are not emerging as a new meta-issue. As the salience of meta-issues declines, the political nonalignment of parties to a dispute becomes less important as a condition of successful conflict management.

The number of serious international disputes is not increasing at a regular rate, but neither is it decreasing. Localized disputes are not more likely to spread now than in earlier eras.

UN decisions have become less forceful. Small mediatory operations are launched as frequently as ever, often successfully. Large observer and peacekeeping operations are mounted less frequently than earlier, and score somewhat less impact.

Effective military operations can be mounted only when the United States and the Soviet Union either favor or do not actively oppose them, though this was not always the case. Effective military operations depend on the availability of national contingents previously earmarked and trained for their missions and on Secretariat procedures for rapidly deploying them.

While, on balance, collective conflict management has kept the world more peaceful than it would otherwise have been, certain international disputes have actually been exacerbated by the UN, notably those in which the label of "racism" was pinned on one of the parties.

Regional organizations have come to compete with the UN and perhaps complicate its work, though this was not always true.

## BEST AND WORST PERFORMANCE OF UN

We know what the UN can do best. It is reasonably effective in abating any kind of dispute not connected with the cold war, and it is often effective in isolating disputes and stopping hostilities in situations of serious fighting, provided the context does not involve East-West issues or a civil war.

We also know the UN's most persistent weakness: it is unable, except in rare circumstances, to settle any dispute with finality. The only qualification of this discouraging conclusion has to do with decolonization conflicts and with some disputes over resources. Eleven crises over such issues were settled, as contrasted with twelve that were not.

Nor are things likely to improve much in the rest of the century. Possibly disputes among members of the same bloc may find their way to the UN more often than in the past because the slow disintegration of cold war alliances makes it more difficult to find satisfaction by appealing to them. The same disintegration may also give the alliance leaders an incentive for permitting the UN to manage disputes among their followers in order to restrain unwanted unilateral moves. But appealing to the UN in such circumstances guarantees no impact on the dispute unless the membership is convinced that the conflicts in question really threaten their interests.*

In fact it seems clear that UN practice has actually made some disputes more intractable than they might have been without UN intervention. The practices that contribute to this condition include the indiscriminate holding of special conferences, the toleration of forum shopping, and the acceptance of a double standard that denounces the use of armed force in general but legitimates it in the case of national liberation against a racist enemy.

Special conferences have the tendency to push one party into a corner, to sigmatize it as the aggressor even if the phrase is not used. They are rhetorical events, not intended to induce negotiations but to provide a propaganda forum for the party enjoying majority support. Such has been the case with respect to Kampuchea, Western Sahara, Namibia, and the Israeli-occupied territories. Each conference gave international legitimacy to a group claiming to be the government but not in actual control of the territory. While governments jealously guard their claim to be the sole legitimate spokesmen for their peoples, the claim is abandoned in the case of the Palestine Liberation Organization, the South West Africa People's Organization, Polisario and the Kampucheans led by Prince Sihanouk.

The same cases also illustrate the negative consequences of forum shopping. In each case the majority was dissatisfied with

---

*These suggestions are made in Finlayson and Zacher.

action taken in the Security Council, even though in cases when the veto was not used some impact might have been scored. Conflicting signals result when cases not dropped from the Security Council agenda are nevertheless shifted to the General Assembly. Institutionalization cannot be expected to occur if this practice is tolerated. Non-state entities are the beneficiaries of the shift, even though their role in a true attempt at settlement is not necessarily improved by the practice. Nor is a settlement brought closer.

These practices are an aspect, in the case of the Arab-Israeli and South African contexts, of the prevalence of a double standard concerning the use of armed force. Armed force is used legitimately, according to the Charter and generally accepted norms, only in self-defense—except in the elimination of "racism." Then it becomes legitimate in the eyes of a UN majority. The evolution of this double standard has made the solution of the Middle East conflict and the elimination of apartheid more intractable by placing blame exclusively on Israel and South Africa. The elimination of colonialism—the major successful achievement of UN peaceful change procedures—has become a justification for war as remaining cases of it are stigmatized as racism. We are back to the practice of distinguishing between just and unjust wars.\*

Kurt Waldheim has recently warned that repeated denunciations of South Africa and Israel do nothing but discredit UN conflict management: "The effect of this activity is to cheapen the currency of UN resolutions and thus to reduce the effectiveness of the United Nations in the peaceful resolution of disputes. . . . The extreme preoccupation of the Organization with a few specific problems of this character, although understandable, is not a healthy one."† It is the wrong kind of politicization because it infects the economic and social programs of the United Nations as well, and thus undercuts them.

These instances raise a basic question: Is it hopeless to expect the UN to deal with the underlying causes of international conflict

---

\*Changes in the law of war further strengthen the argument for the double standard. This is expressed in Protocol I (National Liberation Movements) and the 1977 amendments to the 1949 Geneva Convention, giving belligerent rights to such forces as the PLO, Polisario, and SWAPO. See G.I.A.D. Draper, "Wars of National Liberation and War Criminality," in *Restraints on War*, ed. Michael Howard (London: Oxford University Press, 1979), pp. 135ff.

†"The United Nations: The Tarnished Image," *Foreign Affairs*, Fall 1984, p. 104.

in cases other than simple decolonization? Can the UN only influence the proximate causes of war, and make no basic contribution to the construction of a fundamentally more peaceful world? I now turn to this question by examining the role of the UN in crisis management.

Not all disputes on the agenda of the UN are crises, but crises are the most important kinds of disputes. Crises and crisis management are diagnostic devices in this instance; they enable us to make a judgment on whether the UN can only address the proximate causes of strife. A crisis for a state is "a situational change in its external or internal environment which triggers three interrelated perceptions by its decisionmakers: threat to basic values; a sense of finite time for response to those threats; and a rise in the likelihood of its involvement in some form of military hostilities before the threat has been overcome."* Seventy-one of the disputes submitted to the UN match this definition, even though the three criteria of crisishood were not met to the same degree in all of them.

I now attempt to categorize these crises in terms of whether or not they contained such a threat to basic national values as to represent examples of underlying causes of conflict—rather than particular grievances specific to the countries in question but not indicative of deeper forces in world politics. What would constitute such a threat? If we take the demand for national self-determination and the defense of national selfhood to be a major historical force in evidence since the French Revolution, decolonization disputes that trigger both the strong demand of the colonized and the strong resistance of the colonizer exemplify such a threat and an underlying force. The cold war disputes identify another underlying dimension in evidence since 1917: the systematic confrontation between Communist and anti-Communist countries over a fundamental issue of world order—an issue felt deeply enough to trigger perceptions of

---

*Jonathan Wilkenfeld and Michael Brecher, "International Crises, 1945-1975: The UN Dimension," *International Studies Quarterly* 28 (1984): 47. The results of this study, though the sample of disputes is not identical with mine, generally match my findings in predicting the involvement of the UN and also its impact. Since their study is couched in aggregate terms, however, the pattern of decline over time is not explicated. Their conclusions are as follows (p. 65): 48% of all crises ended in some kind of agreement among the parties, but crises involving UN intervention were more likely to result in an agreement; 60% of all crises resulted in a reduction of tensions, but no relationship between tension reduction and UN involvement could be found; compromise agreements were obtained more often when UN intensive involvement was present.

great threat to national values. Another perennial issue is the security dilemma: the feeling of threat engendered by the mere presence of another state or alliance thought capable of and motivated to eliminate the victim even if nationalism and Communism are not salient motivators. Finally, conflict over a scarce resource can be considered an underlying force in world politics, present many times in history and capable of operating as a motivator for war quite independently of nationalistic, ideological, or security considerations. Faith, greed, pride, and fear, as Hobbes might have said, are the basic causes of war.

The test is this: Is the UN able to handle crises that express these underlying forces as effectively as it handles crises that do not? If so, the impression that the UN, because it is poor at settling disputes with finality, is therefore able to address only the proximate causes of conflict is ill-founded. Table 10 summarizes the experience. By and large the UN is *not* able to address deep-seated causes of conflict unless the issue is nationalism or resources, generally in the context of decolonization. Nationalism and resource-fueled crises among postcolonial states are not dealt with equally effectively. On the other hand, the UN is only slightly more effective in settling crises that involve no other underlying forces. We cannot conclude that the UN excels at dealing with proximate causes of strife while being helpless to undo the basic causes of war. If settlement of crises is the criterion of judgment, the UN is good at neither.

Table 10

ISSUES AND UN SUCCESS IN SETTLING CRISES
*(in percent)*

| Issues | Number | Success in Settlement | | |
|---|---|---|---|---|
| | | None | Limited | Great |
| Nationalism | 16 | 50% | 31% | 19% |
| Cold war | 24 | 87 | 13 | 0 |
| Security | 6 | 100 | 0 | 0 |
| Resources | 7 | 57 | 29 | 14 |
| None | 19 | 74 | 21 | 5 |

Fortunately the fate of the world does not depend on this failing. Whether a given crisis is due to deep causes or merely to the episodic misperceptions of local decisionmakers, a final settlement is not necessary to protect world peace. All crises exhibit the characteristics of proximate causation even if these are also manifestations of deeper sources. Hence the ability to reduce uncertainty, to introduce new information, to provide mediatory channels, and to separate the parties are valuable services in their own right. If they rarely settle the issue, they nevertheless contain the danger by other means. The underlying issues may not vanish, and they tend to reappear in the next crisis. But the Camp David agreements remind us that even this condition need not be permanent. Trends and forces outside the reach of the UN may alter the underlying pattern of causation. In the meantime, by coping with some of their surface manifestations, time is gained and life goes on. Moreover, we can take comfort from the studies of crisis management that show that the underlying causes do not clearly drive the proximate ones. Third-party intervention limited to the proximate causes is often sufficient to head off the most extreme peril.*

This relatively optimistic conclusion is nevertheless a sobering one. Over its forty-year history, the UN's membership managed to agree on and institutionalize *one* new principle: the principle of national self-determination as a basic norm of international order — but only as it applies to liberation from the domination of the industrialized states of the North. One cannot escape the conclusion that most states have become increasingly indifferent to conflict resolution as a basic aim of international life. Tolerance for the nonresolution of many conflicts, or acceptance of a certain amount of permanent conflict, is but the corollary of this weakened belief. It seems most unlikely that such new underlying sources of strife as energy shortages, nuclear proliferation, and the violation of basic human rights constitute concerns of sufficient salience to reverse this trend.†

---

*Compare the contrasting explanations of major crises contained in Nazli Choucri and Robert North, *Nations in Conflict* (San Francisco: W.H. Freeman, 1975), who make the argument that underlying resource issues drive the proximate causes, with Lebow and Snyder and Diesing, who find no such direct link.

†Debra Miller examines the potential that such issues provide the agenda for successful UN intervention in the future, and concludes that most of them will be managed collectively in other forums. Human rights issues can take the place of the declining decolonization issue as a shaper of UN conflict management only if violations can also be shown to be threats to peace. See Miller, "Contributions of the UN to International Security Regimes," in Gati, ed., pp. 131-61.

## POOR INSTITUTIONALIZATION IS NOT THE PROBLEM

Institutional innovations did occur in the life of the United Nations. Many of them survived the shift from the concert, to permissive enforcement with balancing, to permissive engagement, and back again. In fact, these shifts are a reflection of institutional innovations. However, we have to ask whether changes in the rules and procedures contained in the Charter make for more or for less predictability in conduct. Institutionalization implies regularity, order, and predictability. Relaxing the original practices may also imply the abandonment of order and the emergence of improvisation, all justified in the name of flexibility. Changes have to be judged in terms of their presumed ability to make conflict management more effective.

Some innovations undoubtedly have had this result. The most prominent are the practices associated with permissive engagement and peacekeeping. Paradoxically, they were made possible by the earlier innovations of permissive enforcement and the Uniting for Peace resolution which weakened the role of the Security Council, even though permissive enforcement also had the effect of making the UN the appendage of the United States and of alienating the Soviet Union. One could conclude that the Hammarskjöld innovations repaired the damage done by Uniting for Peace while exploiting the earlier innovation for a new advance in institutionalization. In any event, the demise of big power standby forces and of the Military Staff Committee were regretted by few. Nor was the sparing invocation of articles 39 and 40 and the abandonment of the stylized steps for the peaceful settlement of disputes of chapter 6. All of these constitute adaptive innovations.

So do the voting customs that have evolved in the Security Council. Less contentious consensus formation has been facilitated by the abandonment of the rule that abstention by a permanent member constitutes a veto, and by the demise of the double veto. The recognized role of the Council president in fashioning "consensus" decisions that avoid voting altogether is a similar development. And so is the unchallenged power of the Secretary-General to take a prominent position in conflict management, though the extent of the prominence remains an issue.

Other institutional changes, however, have had the opposite effect. The growing legitimacy of the General Assembly in conflict management, introduced by the practice of permissive enforcement, tends to produce more divisiveness than action. It has made possible the double standard for judging threats to the peace which has bedevilled conflict management. The Charter orders parties to a dispute, if they are members of the Security Council, to abstain from voting under chapter 6; the permanent members have failed to abide by this rule. The most de-institutionalizing innovation of all is the dispute over the obligatory financing of peacekeeping operations. It exemplifies the incompleteness of the consensus about the earlier innovations relating to the powers of the Secretary-General and the General Assembly. It underscores the fact that permissive engagement has not been successfully institutionalized.

Can it be? It seems exceedingly doubtful. The failure of complete institutional reform in the direction of flexible adaptation is not due to a lack of legal imagination or administrative skill.* It is due to the fact that the UN is and always has been viewed by its members as an instrument of national foreign policy. As the number of voting blocs increases and as the interests of their members diverge further, there are more sets of national interests to be brought under a single hat. Winning coalitions become more difficult to build, especially as there are fewer meta-issues around which a stable consensus can develop. Hence innovations are advocated when they seem to serve the purpose of national policy, and they are abandoned when they no longer appear useful. The salience of the UN to the advancement of whatever national interests are funnelled into the organization determines adaptive success.

This explanation also assumes that the early successes of the United Nations are largely explicable in terms of the importance of alignments. While effective conflict management could not be expected in situations pitting the opposing cold war coalitions against one another, conflict management was quite possible when a member of one alignment faced a nonaligned antagonist. Moreover, this explanation suggests that UN effectiveness would remain respectable as long as the parties to dispute are superpowers, large powers,

---

*One modest institutional change might nevertheless be considered, though it requires an amendment to the Charter. It has been suggested that the ability of the Secretary-General to take prominent action in conflict management is sometimes limited by his fear of alienating member states whose votes he needs for reelection. This could be avoided by extending his term of office to seven or eight years and limiting each incumbent to one term. Such a rule would not have saved Trygve Lie from the wrath of the Soviet Union, but it would have protected Hammarskjöld and given Waldheim an inducement to act more decisively. It seems as if Perez de Cuellar is acting in the spirit of this suggestion.

or smaller states under the diplomatic and military influence of a superpower. Most third world states, however, escape these constraints. Their increasing numbers would thus complicate conflict management because they are not reliable coalition partners and do not necessarily share the objectives of other states sufficiently to be part of a stable consensus.

Figure 9 gives considerable support to this explanation. It shows that while the main nonimplementers of UN decisions were, until 1970, the members of cold war alignments, this is no longer true. Now the nonaligned middle and smaller powers are almost as often the culprits. The curve confirms that in the most recent periods the earlier explanatory power of alignments in predicting UN involvement *and* UN success no longer holds. The diplomatic and military texture of the world has perhaps grown too complex for effective collective security practices.

This explanation is, in turn, entirely consistent with the notion that effectiveness is associated with a small number of meta-issues around which consensus can be built. Once these meta-issues lose their relevance, and if no new overarching concern develops, conflict management becomes less effective.

Figure 9 confirms this hypothesis. Decay is associated with the advent of nonaligned smaller states as the main antagonists, as it is with the increasing incidence of issues other than decolonization and the cold war. The successes scored by the United Nations before 1970 were heavily concentrated on managing conflicts associated with colonial liberation movements. Now few remain, and they are recalcitrant cases. Global conflict may be increasing, but the issues over which countries disagree no longer fit the earlier categories.

## LEARNING, RATIONALITY, AND THE EVOLUTION OF RECIPROCITY

The more impatient and apocalyptically minded may easily come to the conclusion that the UN's record means that the world has reached a point of no return. The initial design has not worked. The many institutional innovations made since have not sufficed to make matters dramatically better. Tinkering with the original design by making incremental adjustments is not enough. The very innovations have created so much "noise" in the conflict management system that no clear "signal" can be expected to emerge. Therefore, it might be argued, the UN has reached a point of no

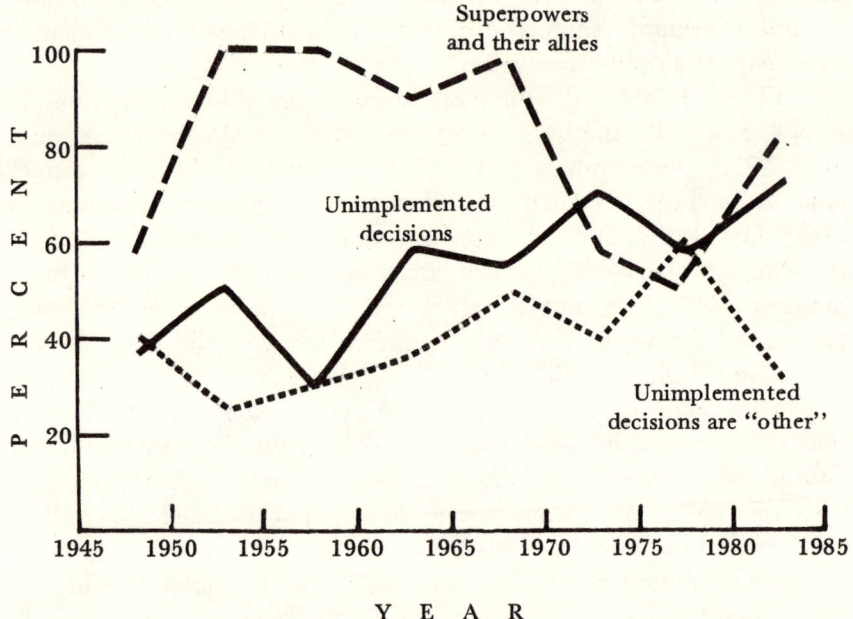

Figure 9. NONIMPLEMENTERS OF SUBSTANTIVE UN DECISIONS
*(N = 53)*

*Source:* Appendix B, Table G

return. A totally new organization must be designed, or the world must do without one.

To argue in these terms implies a belief in the wit of man to design his own future by creating effective institutions. It opts for the kind of rationality that stresses consensus on means and ignores dissensus on ends. Technical, or practical, rationality (as in cost-benefit calculations) stipulates agreement on the end to be served by a choice and provides the decision-rules for finding the most effective and efficient means toward that end. The deliberate design of better institutions requires this view of what consitutes rational choice. It also implies an inordinate optimism about transcending the burdens of history.

There are weighty objections to such a view. I contrast it with an evolutionary interpretation of politics, which presupposes some rough political analog to the idea of natural selection. Whatever evolved, whatever mankind has contrived for its governance, evolved for some reason. Whatever evolved, including the UN's conflict management machinery, must have had survival value for international society. Otherwise it would have been abandoned years ago, or mankind would have destroyed itself in a third world war. Conflict management by multilateral means, in short, is an adaptive trait that has enabled mankind to occupy and penetrate a large number of "niches." The inference is clear: don't undo with new institutional tinkering something that came about for a good reason. The reason is the normal behavior of states which cannot be expected to change in the near future. The ecological constraints and opportunities that account for this behavior are long-lived. While they last, we must live with the international institutions that have evolved.

This fatalistic view, whatever one may think of its debt to natural science, is also subject to weighty objections even for those who do not expect an apocalypse. What caused the original design of an institution, since it surely did not evolve according to genetic principles? Despite ecological constraints, states do change their behavior. The fact that the security dilemma persists need not carry with it the inference that the dilemma must be, and always has been, met by the same behavioral patterns. In fact, behavioral adaption may have a much larger role in biological evolution than has been suspected. If this is so, then a change in "consciousness" is possible. Hence institutional utopianism should not be so sharply juxtaposed to historical inevitability.

My position is intermediate between these extremes. As Marx said, men do make their own future, but they do not make it exactly as they wish. Volition and constraint interact; they do not stalemate each other. If all volitions agreed on the shape of a desired order, if harmony on values actually existed, technical rationality could rule. The major constraint facing such a course of action, however, is that men and their governments *do not agree* on the values that ought to guide the design of the institutions which could lead to a different world order. Technical rationality alone will not serve in this situation. What Max Weber called value rationality must prevail as well; more important, agreement on institutional improvement presupposes a single value rationality for all major nations, instead of the competing value rationalities which prevail today.

Given this situation, the question of whether improved conflict management institutions are possible cannot be answered without asking a prior question. Have governments learned anything about peace and conflict avoidance *despite* the prevalence of competing values during the last forty years? If they have, then the lessons have shaped the volitions of governments and overcome some of the constraints of the dilemma of insecurity *despite* the continued imperfection of the UN. We would have to conclude that the world can continue to live with those imperfections.

But even this conclusion cannot be reached without asking another prior question. The world can be expected to put up with imperfect conflict management system only if the actual state of insecurity today is *not* worse that it was in 1945 or 1950 or 1960. If it is worse, then the overall danger to survival would negate any tolerance of imperfection, irrespective of our understanding of its causes. In what ways, then, is today's world more or less secure than in the recent past?

There is *less* security now than before 1960 for small nonaligned third world states engaging in low-level conflict with their neighbors. The rest of the world tolerates such conflict without undue worry over escalation or local damage. Moreover, the decline in security for weak and nonaligned African and Asian states exposed to intervention from their neighbors, because it does not endanger the rest of the world, has no marked malign impact on the stability of the international system as a whole. National security suffers while international security remains unharmed.

This, however, is not true for all small states. Third world countries who enjoy the protection of some extraregional hegemon

(Angola, Morocco, El Salvador) escape the condition just described and probably enjoy *more* security now than earlier. Small states in western and eastern Europe are clearly far *more* secure today than in the interwar period and before, for reasons too well known to require recapitulation.

There is *more* security than earlier with respect to serious disputes among middle and smaller states. When there is a danger of escalation in such conflicts, third-party intercession is practiced with consistency and considerable success, though not often to the point of removing the grievance from the international agenda altogether.

There is *less* security than earlier with respect to the relations among states with nuclear arsenals. Horizontal and vertical nuclear proliferation poses new dangers to security in the future, unless we make the dangerous assumption that the prudent rules of self-restraint practiced by the United States and the Soviet Union will be adopted by all and prevail forever. The escalation of the technological arms race between the superpowers poses the same danger. The failure of post-1945 efforts at disarmament and arms control, a failure quite unrelated to the institutional imperfections of the UN, lessens everybody's security.

I offer the conclusion that something has been learned. Learning has not taken the form of the deliberate design of more effective practices. Governments have stumbled onto the lessons without changing their basic values and without practicing technical rationality. They have stumbled into the mutual recognition of serious constraints on their freedom of action to make war under circumstances which in the past led to hostilities. The constraints include the kind of counter-pressure and the mediatory services made available on the East River.

Eventually the recognition of the constraints can lead to new definitions of problems facing peace—definitions that include an appreciation for the underlying causes of war. Finally, new definitions of problems can lead to new routines for solving the problems. These things have happened in the economic sphere, in public health, in telecommunications, in the work of the specialized agencies, of UNCTAD, of UNIDO. They have not yet happened in the realm of conflict management. There the constraints are recognized, but the redefinition of the problem has not yet occurred.

What, then, has been learned? There has been little internalization of discrete lessons from past experience. All the "errors" of judgment in decision-making to which cognitive psychology calls attention continue to be made. There is no institutional memory of great power. Each generation of national and international decision-makers seems to be condemned to relearn the same old lessons. There has been little institutional learning because the changes in decision-making reflected in the four phases of UN institutional life have never been finally routinized. If learning means the collective mastering of a task by profiting from prior trial-and-error or stimulus-response experiences, the world's use of the UN spells failure.

But suppose we think about learning in a different way, following the literature on collective action.* Actors, being out to win, are preoccupied with the short run only. Their attitude toward institutions is opportunistic. They cannot be assumed to welcome the help of third parties, show good will, be eager to settle.† From the viewpoint of defining and implementing a permanent collective good—international peace—their behavior is irrational, though from the perspective of safeguarding a private good it is not. Yet a sequence of episodes involving conflict and its abatement through the UN can also be expected to make actors aware of the fact that they are subject to constraints other than their relative weakness vis-à-vis their opponents. Such constraints include the need to justify themselves when attacked in a UN forum, to be threatened with boycotts or ostracism, to be made the subject of peacekeeping against their will. The constraints also include the recognition that persistence in unilateral behavior can result in eventual isolation and even defeat.

In short, states devoid of altruism can reasonably be expected to become aware of their enmeshment in a situation of strategic interdependence, of mutual awareness that their moves depend

---

*The remainder of my argument is eclectic and owes a great deal to a number of authors concerned with rational choice in international relations. I am particularly indebted to Russell Hardin, *Collective Action* (Baltimore: Johns Hopkins University Press, 1982); Robert Axelrod, *The Evolution of Cooperation* (New York: Basic Books, 1984); Snyder and Diesing, chs. 2 and 3; Robert O. Keohane, "Reciprocity in International Relations," *International Organization* 40, 1 (Winter 1986); Robert Jervis, "Cooperation under the Security Dilemma," *World Politics*, January 1978; John G. Cross, "Negotiation as a Learning Process," in *The Negotiation Process*, ed. I. William Zartmann (Beverly Hills: Sage Publications, 1978).

†The case that these qualities are essential ingredients of effective international conflict management is made by Jacob Bercovitch, *Social Conflict and Third Parties* (Boulder: Westview, 1984).

on how they perceive the perceptions of the antagonist, whose array of options depends on the same double calculation. The policy implication of this constraint is the maxim "Don't push too hard," under conditions of potential later danger and under considerable uncertainty. Paradoxically, this system of interaction imposes rationality on otherwise irrational states. The obverse is also true: if strategic interdependence is weak, so are the constraints on the realization of private goods. In such a case, no learning will take place. The real world of conflict management seems to represent both patterns. To the extent that things could be much worse, compared to conflict before 1945, systemic learning has taken place. The fact that it is not cumulative, not equally internalized by all states, and subject to reversals should remind us of the fragility of this learning process.

Let us now suspend disbelief and follow the logic of continuing systemic learning a little longer. What else could be learned to make conflict management more institutionalized? Eventually even the lessons of systemic learning have to be assimilated by living bureaucrats and politicians to become permanent. In the language of game theory, the players in the security game must be conscious of the advantage of collaborating, instead of defecting, even though their communication remains tacit. Implicit and uncodified rules of the game must become explicitly recognized.

Game theory shows that this is indeed possible. Repeated experiments have shown that in iterated games such a recognition can emerge as the most beneficial strategy for both players—still subject to reversal. Whether such a process can be experimentally demonstrated in a situation involving more than two players remains to be seen. Nevertheless, if real-life conflict management contains an analogous learning process, it is not unreasonable to expect an actor who has learned this lesson in one encounter to remember it in the next conflict, provided his expectation of a reward for such behavior is actually met. We must recall that learned cooperative behavior is not a selfless act: it depends on being rewarded.

Prisoner-dilemma gaming, from which this argument is extracted, is not the only kind of game mirroring international conflict behavior. Various types of real conflicts and the expectations of the actors correspond to a variety of games, more or less dangerous, not equally likely to yield to cooperation. Making them into cooperative games in all cases involves a cognitive adjustment as well as a systemic constraint. Each player must "correct" his initial misestimate of his opponent's preference schedule. Arriving at cooperative solutions seems to require a constant reexamination of one's own appraisal of how the opponent ranks his objectives. A bargain can be struck when the two learning curves intersect. Institutional growth can occur when the lessons of several of these bargaining encounters are assembled and mentally codified, provided the perceived constraints remain constant or become tighter. This did not happen consistently in the life of the UN; not all constraints met this condition for all parties.

But a close study of bilateral and mediated crisis management not involving international organizations shows that governments are capable of behaving in such a fashion. They can, under the optimal circumstances just described, transform a dangerous game into a less dangerous one. Diplomatic history studied from the vantage point of game theory has shown that governments do not always consider noncooperation—even if it was the initial strategy—to be the final and best strategy. This is a possibility, not a certainty. Making governments progressively cooperative requires that the likelihood of a reward be increased. This brings us to the principle of reciprocity.

Reciprocity in interpersonal and in interstate relations involves four ingredients. The principle of *obligation* presumes the existence of a framework of fairness, a shared sense of what constitutes proper behavior, a sense of acceptable and unacceptable conduct. This is closely linked to the idea of *contingency*—the idea that like acts bring like responses, that good is met with good and bad with bad. Reciprocity also implies *sequentiality:* no immediate reward need be expected for a concession, the benefits from an exchange can be deferred by one or both parties as long as concessions are eventually made. Gratification can be delayed. The idea of *equivalence* suggests that concessions need not be of equal value at the time they are made. Delayed gratification also implies that later in the sequence equivalence of benefits will come about, permitting one or both parties to forego it at the time of the initial exchange. Institutional learning would seem to require the acceptance of both sequentiality and equivalence as essential ingredients.

Has such a concept of reciprocity developed in the UN? Perhaps it has in the economic and social realm, but not in the sphere of conflict management. The sense of obligation is weak; the prevalent expectations about contingency suggest that "bads" outweigh the "goods." Sequentiality and equivalence are practiced only intermittently, though the willingness of certain states to bear heavy peacekeeping costs implies a bet on some future successes, a deferral of immediate gratification and a disregard for a response of equal value. Certain states demonstrate the required pattern of behavior, but not enough of them to enable us to claim that reciprocity has been enshrined as an overall norm of conduct that lays the basis for further institutional learning.

To argue that everybody should immediately practice reciprocity is to expect the leopard to lose his spots. We must wait for relationships of constraint to develop which will trigger the process gradually. Sufficient reciprocity now exists to permit the management of the proximate causes of conflict in situations considered serious threats to peace. Not enough exists to permit the UN's conflict management machinery to address the underlying causes as well. These are tackled in other forums of the United Nations, slowly but unmistakably. Whether they will change mutual expectations enough to remove or weaken the deep-seated sources of conflict in time is uncertain. But in the meantime we ought to rejoice that enough has been learned to permit the control of some very nasty threats to the peace. The evolution of human consciousness does not depend on the geologic time scales of biological evolution, but it takes more than forty years.

# APPENDIXES

## Appendix A

## REFERRALS OF INTERNATIONAL DISPUTES, 1945-1984

### DISPUTES REFERRED TO THE UNITED NATIONS

| Date | Dispute | Parties | Intensity | Impact |
|---|---|---|---|---|
| 1945-49 | Corfu Channel | Albania, UK | Low | Some |
| 1945-49 | Indonesian independence | Netherlands, Indonesia | High | Great |
| 1946-51 | Greek civil war | Greece, US, UK, USSR, Bulgaria, Yugoslavia, Albania | Very high | Moderate |
| 1946 | Azerbaijan | US, USSR, Iran | Low | Moderate |
| 1946 | French in Levant | France, UK, Syria Lebanon | Insignificant | Some |
| 1946- | Status of Namibia | South Africa, most African states | High | Some |
| 1946-62 | Indians in South Africa | South Africa, India | Low | None |
| 1947-53 | Status of Trieste | Yugoslavia, US, UK USSR, (Italy) | Very low | None |
| 1947-49 | Palestine independence | Israel, Arab states | High | Moderate |
| 1947 | Future of Sudan | UK, Egypt | Insignificant | None |
| 1947-50 | Korean unification | USSR, US | Moderate | None |
| 1947-56 | Future of Togoland | UK (Ghana), Ewes | Very low | Great |
| 1947-48 | Kashmir secession | India, Pakistan | Moderate | Moderate |
| 1948 | Czech coup* | Czechoslovakia, USSR | Low | None |

*Referral was purely symbolic; circumstances made any real organizational impact impossible. Not counted in statistical compilations.

Appendix A *(continued):* United Nations

| Date | Dispute | Parties | Intensity | Impact |
|---|---|---|---|---|
| 1948-49 | Russian wives | US, USSR | Insignificant | Some |
| 1948 | Status of Hyderabad* | India, Hyderabad | Moderate | None |
| 1948 | Berlin blockade | USSR, US, UK, France | Very low | None |
| 1948-51 | Soviet-Yugoslav rift | USSR, Yugoslavia | Low | None |
| 1949-50 | East European human rights* | US, Bolivia, Australia, all East European states | Insignificant | None |
| 1949-51 | Status of Cyrenaica | Italy, France, US, UK, Arab states | Low | Great |
| 1949-56 | Palestine truce | Israel, Egypt, Jordan Syria, Lebanon | High | Some |
| 1949-64 | Kashmir negotiations | India, Pakistan | High | Moderate |
| 1950-51 | Korean war | US et al., USSR, China, South Korea, North Korea | Very high | None |
| 1950 | Action of US 7th Fleet | US, China | Insignificant | None |
| 1950 | Tibetan aggression* | China, Tibet | Low | None |
| 1951-55 | Moroccan independence | France, Egypt (Morocco) | Low | None |
| 1951-64 | Somali border | Italy (Somalia), Kenya, Ethiopia | Moderate | None |
| 1951 | German unification* | USSR, US, UK, France | Moderate | None |
| 1951-53 | Iran oil nationalization | Iran, UK | Very low | None |
| 1951-53 | Korean negotiations | US, USSR, China, South Korea, North Korea | Very high | Great |
| 1952-56 | Tunisian independence | France, Arab states | Low | None |

Appendix A *(continued):* United Nations

| Date | Dispute | Parties | Intensity | Impact |
|---|---|---|---|---|
| 1953-57 | US intervention in East Europe* | US, USSR, Czechoslovakia | Very low | None |
| 1953 | Kuomintang in Burma | Burma, Taiwan | High | Great |
| 1954 | Threat to Thailand | Thailand, North Vietnam | Insignificant | None |
| 1954 | Guatemalan civil war | Guatemala, US, Honduras | Very low | None |
| 1954 | Siberian air incident* | US, USSR | Insignificant | None |
| 1954-62 | Status of West Irian | Indonesia, Netherlands | Low | Great |
| 1954 | China Seas piracy | USSR, Taiwan | Insignificant | Some |
| 1954-58 | Status of Cyprus | UK, Turkey, Greece | Low | None |
| 1954-55 | Chinese offshore islands | China, US, Taiwan | Very low | None |
| 1955-62 | Algerian independence | France, Arab states | Very high | Some |
| 1956 | Suez war | Egypt, Israel, UK, France | High | Great |
| 1956 | Hungarian intervention | USSR, Hungary | High | None |
| 1957-67 | Palestine borders | Israel, Egypt, Syria Jordan | High | Some |
| 1957-63 | British Cameroon | UK (Nigeria), France (Cameroun) | Low | Great |
| 1957 | Turkish/Syrian border | Turkey, Syria | Insignificant | None |
| 1958 | Sakiet raid | Tunisia, France | Insignificant | Moderate |
| 1958 | Wadi Halfa | Sudan, Egypt | Insignificant | Some |
| 1958 | Lebanon/Jordan civil war | US, UK, UAR, Jordan, Lebanon | Very low | Moderate |
| 1959-60 | Thai/Cambodian border | Thailand, Cambodia | Very low | Great |

Appendix A *(continued):* United Nations

| Date | Dispute | Parties | Intensity | Impact |
|---|---|---|---|---|
| 1959-60 | Buraimi oasis | UK, Saudi Arabia | Insignificant | Some |
| 1959-62 | Laos civil war | US, USSR, Laos | Very high | Some |
| 1959-65 | Treatment of Tibet | China, Tibet | Moderate | None |
| 1960 | U-2 incident* | US, USSR | Insignificant | None |
| 1960 | Eichmann abduction* | Israel, Argentina | Insignificant | Great |
| 1960 | RB-47 incident* | US, USSR | Insignificant | None |
| 1960-63 | Zaire independence | Belgium, Zaire, African states | Very high | Great |
| 1960-61 | US threats to Cuba* | US, Cuba | Low | None |
| 1960-61 | South Tyrol | Austria, Italy | Insignificant | None |
| 1960-61 | Moroccan/Mauritanian border | Morocco, Mauritania | Insignificant | Some |
| 1961-74 | Portuguese colonies in Africa | Portugal, all African states | High | None |
| 1961 | Bay of Pigs* | US, Cuba | Low | None |
| 1961 | Kuwait independence | UK, Iraq | Very low | Some |
| 1961 | Bizerta | Tunisia, France | Moderate | Moderate |
| 1961-70 | Oman civil war | UK (Muscat), Arab states (Oman) | Moderate | None |
| 1961 | Goa | India, Portugal | Very low | None |
| 1962 | Cuban missile crisis | US, USSR (Cuba) | High | None |
| 1962-76 | Repression in South Africa | South Africa, all African states | High | None |
| 1962-65 | Guyana independence | UK, Guyana | Low | None |
| 1962-67 | Yemen civil war | Egypt, Saudi Arabia | High | None |
| 1962 | Guyana border | Venezuela, UK | Insignificant | None |

Appendix A (continued): United Nations

| Date | Dispute | Parties | Intensity | Impact |
|---|---|---|---|---|
| 1963 | Vietnamese Buddhists* | South Vietnam, 14 African states | Insignificant | None |
| 1963-65 | South African High Commission territories | UK, South Africa | Low | Great |
| 1963-74 | Portuguese Guinea | Portugal, Senegal | High | None |
| 1963 | Intervention in Haiti | Haiti, Dominican Republic | Insignificant | None |
| 1963 | Malaysian confrontation | Indonesia, Malaysia | Low | None |
| 1963 | Status of Sarawak/Sabah | Indonesia, Malaysia, Philippines | Insignificant | Some |
| 1963-68 | Aden independence | UK, Yemen | Moderate | Moderate |
| 1963-73 | Cyprus civil war | Cyprus, Greece, Turkey | Moderate | Great |
| 1963-79 | Rhodesian independence | Rhodesia, UK, African states | High | Some |
| 1963-64 | Tutsi restoration attempt | Rwanda, Burundi | Moderate | Some |
| 1964 | Panama Canal 1 | US, Panama | Insignificant | Some |
| 1964-66 | Aden/Yemen border | UK, Yemen | Low | None |
| 1964-67 | Cambodian border* | Cambodia, US, South Vietnam | Low | None |
| 1964 | Persecution of Greeks | Greece, Turkey | Insignificant | None |
| 1964- | Status of Gibraltar | Spain, UK | Very low | None |
| 1964-75 | Spanish Sahara independence | Spain, Morocco, Mauritania | Moderate | None |
| 1964-69 | Ifni | Spain, Morocco | Very low | Great |
| 1964 | Stanleyville air rescue* | US, Belgium, Zaire, African states | Low | None |

78     Appendix A

Appendix A *(continued)*: United Nations

| Date | Dispute | Parties | Intensity | Impact |
|---|---|---|---|---|
| 1965 | US intervention in Dominican Republic | US, USSR, Dominican factions | Low | None |
| 1965-82 | Status of Falkland Islands | UK, Argentina | Very low | Some |
| 1965-70 | 2nd Kashmir war and negotiations | Pakistan, India | High | Moderate |
| 1965-74 | Vietnam war | US, South Vietnam, North Vietnam, (USSR) | Very high | None |
| 1966-68 | Katanga exiles | Portugal, Zaire | Very low | Some |
| 1967 | Six-Day war | Israel, Egypt, Syria, Jordan | Very high | Moderate |
| 1967-73 | Arab-Israeli confrontation | Israel, Egypt, Syria, Jordan | High | Some |
| 1967-77 | Djibouti independence | France, Somalia | Low | Moderate |
| 1967 | Battle of the hostages* | Ivory Coast, Guinea | Insignificant | None |
| 1968 | Pueblo incident | US, North Korea | Very low | None |
| 1968 | Exiles in Haiti* | US, Haiti | Insignificant | None |
| 1968 | Intervention in Czechoslovakia* | USSR, Czechoslovakia | Insignificant | None |
| 1969-75 | Persian Gulf access | Iran, Iraq | High | Great |
| 1969 | Equatorial Guinea | Equatorial Guinea, Spain | Insignificant | Some |
| 1969-74 | Zambia/Mozambique border | Portugal, Zambia | Moderate | None |
| 1969-70 | Guinea/Portugal border (Conakry raid) | Portugal, Guinea | Moderate | None |
| 1970 | Bahrein independence | UK, Iran | Very low | Some |
| 1970-72 | Eritrean independence | Ethiopia, Arab states | High | None |

Appendix A *(continued):* United Nations

| Date | Dispute | Parties | Intensity | Impact |
|---|---|---|---|---|
| 1971 | Bangladesh independence | India, Pakistan | Moderate | None |
| 1971-79 | Rhodesia/Zambia border | Rhodesia, Zambia, South Africa | High | None |
| 1971-78 | Panama Canal 2 | US, Panama | Low | Some |
| 1973 | Yom Kippur war | Israel, Egypt, Syria | Very high | Great |
| 1973- | Puerto Rican independence | US, Cuba, Iraq, Syria | Low | None |
| 1973 | Mayotte secession | France, Guinea-Bissau et al. | Very low | None |
| 1973 | Chilean revolution | Chile, Cuba | Insignificant | None |
| 1974 | Cyprus invasion | Turkey, Greece, Cyprus | Low | Great |
| 1974- | Cyprus negotiations | Turkey, Greece, Cyprus | Very low | Moderate |
| 1974- | Chilean repression | Chile, everybody | Moderate | Some |
| 1974-77 | Aegean Sea delimitation | Greece, Turkey | Low | None |
| 1975 | Timor independence | Indonesia, Timor | High | None |
| 1975-81 | Belize independence | Belize (UK), Guatemala | Low | Some |
| 1976 | Farakka barrage | India, Bangladesh | Insignificant | Some |
| 1976- | Chad border | Chad, Libya | Moderate | None |
| 1976 | Transkei border | South Africa, Lesotho | Low | Some |
| 1976- | South African persecutions | South Africa, African states | High | Some |
| 1976- | Western Sahara war | Algeria, Morocco, Polisario | High | Some |

Appendix A *(continued):* United Nations

| Date | Dispute | Parties | Intensity | Impact |
|---|---|---|---|---|
| 1976- | Israeli-occupied territories | Israel, PLO,$^a$ Jordan, Syria | High | Some |
| 1976 | Djibouti kidnappings* | France, Somalia | Insignificant | None |
| 1976 | Entebbe raid* | Israel, Uganda | Insignificant | None |
| 1976- | Attacks on Angola | South Africa, Angola, SWAPO$^b$ | High | Some |
| 1977 | Benin coup | Benin, mercenaries, Morocco (?) | Very low | Some |
| 1977-79 | Rhodesia/Botswana border | Rhodesia, Botswana | Moderate | None |
| 1977-79 | Rhodesia/Mozambique border | Rhodesia, Mozambique | High | None |
| 1978 | Sandinista revolt | Costa Rica, Venezuela, Nicaragua | Very low | None |
| 1978 | Litani River war | Israel, PLO$^a$ | High | Moderate |
| 1978 | Burmese refugees | Burma, Bangladesh | Insignificant | Some |
| 1979- | Kampuchea invasion | Kampuchea, Vietnam | High | None |
| 1979-82 | Israeli raids in Lebanon | Israel, Lebanon, Syria, PLO$^a$ | High | Some |
| 1979-80 | New Hebrides independence | Local factions, France, UK | Insignificant | Moderate |
| 1979-81 | US hostages in Iran | US, Iran | Moderate | Some |
| 1979- | Sino-Vietnam border | China, Vietnam | Moderate | None |
| 1979- | Malagasy Islands, | Madagascar, France | Insignificant | None |
| 1980- | Human rights in El Salvador | El Salvador, several Communist countries | High | Some |

$^a$Palestine Liberation Organization
$^b$South West Africa People's Organization

Appendix A *(continued):* United Nations

| Date | Dispute | Parties | Intensity | Impact |
|---|---|---|---|---|
| 1980-82 | Maltese sea boundary | Libya, Malta | Insignificant | Moderate |
| 1980- | Persian Gulf war | Iran, Iraq | High | Some |
| 1980- | Afghanistan intervention | USSR, Afghan factions | High | Some |
| 1981 | Baghdad reactor raid | Israel, Iraq | Insignificant | Some |
| 1981- | Gulf of Sidra | Libya, US | Low | None |
| 1981 | Seychelles invasion | Seychelles, South Africa | Insignificant | Some |
| 1982 | Maseru raid | Lesotho, South Africa | Low | None |
| 1982- | Anti-Sandinista revolt—north | Nicaragua, Honduras, US | High | None |
| 1982- | Essequibo | Guyana, Venezuela | Insignificant | Some |
| 1982 | Falkland Islands war | Argentina, UK | Moderate | Some |
| 1982-83 | Beirut invasion | Israel, Syria, PLO[a] | High | None |
| 1983 | Korean jetliner | USSR, US | Insignificant | None |
| 1983- | Aouzou strip | Chad, Libya | Low | None |
| 1983 | Grenada invasion | US, Nicaragua | Low | None |
| 1984 | Corinto mining | US, Nicaragua | Insignificant | Some |
| 1984 | Occupation of South Lebanon | Israel, Lebanon | Low | None |

## DISPUTES REFERRED TO THE LEAGUE OF ARAB STATES

| Date | Dispute | Parties | Intensity | Impact |
|---|---|---|---|---|
| 1950 | Jordanian expansion | Jordan, other Arab states | Insignificant | None |
| 1955-56 | Baghdad pact | Iraq, Syria, Egypt | Insignificant | None |
| 1955 | Buraimi oasis | Saudi Arabia, Trucial states (UK) | Insignificant | None |
| 1958 | Wadi Halfa | Egypt, Sudan | Insignificant | None |
| 1958-61 | Ben Yussef asylum | Tunisia, UAR | Insignificant | None |
| 1958 | Lebanon/Jordan civil wars | Lebanon, Jordan, UAR, (US, UK) | Very low | Some |
| 1959-61 | Nasser-Kassim feud* | UAR, Iraq | Very low | None |
| 1959-62 | Jordan/UAR tensions | Jordan, UAR | Very low | None |
| 1961-63 | Kuwait independence | Iraq, Kuwait (UK) | Very low | Great |
| 1961 | UAR breakup | Syria, Egypt, Lebanon | Very low | Some |
| 1962-67 | Yemen civil war | Egypt, Saudi Arabia, Yemeni factions | High | None |
| 1963 | Algerian/Moroccan border | Algeria, Morocco | Moderate | None |
| 1970-71 | Jordan civil war | Jordan, Syria, PLO,[a] (Israel) | Very high | Some |
| 1972 | Yemen border 1 | North Yemen, South Yemen, (Saudi Arabia) | Moderate | Great |
| 1974 | Dhofar rebellion | Oman, South Yemen, (Iran, UK) | High | Some |
| 1975 | Euphrates waters | Iraq, Syria | Insignificant | None |
| 1976-77 | Libyan-Egyptian tensions | Egypt, Libya | Low | None |

Appendix A *(continued):* Arab League

| Date | Dispute | Parties | Intensity | Impact |
|---|---|---|---|---|
| 1976- | Western Sahara war | Algeria, Morocco, Mauritania, (Libya) | High | None |
| 1976-78 | Attempted Sudanese coup | Sudan, Libya | Low | None |
| 1976- | Lebanese civil war | Syria, Lebanese factions, (US, Israel) | High | Some |
| 1977 | Gabes dispute | Tunisia, Libya | Very low | Some |
| 1978-79 | Yemen border 2 | South Yemen, North Yemen | Moderate | Great |
| 1979-80 | Gafsa incident | Tunisia, Libya, (France) | Low | Some |
| 1981-82 | Dhofar border† | Oman, South Yemen | Insignificant | Great |
| 1982- | Hanai Island† | Qatar, Bahrein | Insignificant | Moderate |

†Referred to Gulf Cooperation Council

## Appendix A

### DISPUTES REFERRED TO THE ORGANIZATION OF AMERICAN STATES (OAS)

| Date | Dispute | Parties | Intensity | Impact |
|---|---|---|---|---|
| 1948-49 | Costa Rican exiles 1 | Costa Rica, Nicaragua | Insignificant | Great |
| 1949 | Dominican moral aggression | Dominican Republic, Haiti | Insignificant | Some |
| 1950-51 | Caribbean plots | Dominican Republic, Haiti, Cuba | Very low | Some |
| 1951 | Cuban sailors | Dominican Republic, Cuba | Insignificant | Great |
| 1953-54 | Haya de la Torre asylum | Peru, Colombia | Insignificant | None |
| 1954 | Arbenz ouster | Guatemala, US | Very low | Some |
| 1955 | Costa Rican exiles 2 | Costa Rica, Nicaragua | Very low | Great |
| 1955 | Peru-Ecuador border 1 | Peru, Ecuador | Insignificant | Some |
| 1957-61 | Honduran border | Honduras, Nicaragua | Low | Great |
| 1959 | Panamanian revolutionaries | Panama, Cuba | Insignificant | Moderate |
| 1959 | Nicaraguan exiles* | Nicaragua, Costa Rica | Insignificant | None |
| 1959 | Revolutionaries in Dominican Republic | Dominican Republic, Cuba, Venezuela | Insignificant | None |
| 1959 | Invasion of Haiti | Haiti, Cuba | Insignificant | Some |
| 1960 | Asylum for Dominicans | Dominican Republic, Ecuador | Insignificant | None |
| 1960-62 | Ostracism of Cuba | Cuba, US | Low | None |
| 1960-62 | Dominican tyranny | Dominican Republic, Venezuela, US | Low | Moderate |
| 1961 | Mexican border | Mexico, Guatemala | Insignificant | Great |
| 1962- | Laura River diversion | Bolivia, Chile | Very low | Some |

## Appendix A *(continued):* OAS

| Date | Dispute | Parties | Intensity | Impact |
|---|---|---|---|---|
| 1963 | Haitian tyranny | Haiti, US | Insignificant | Some |
| 1963-67 | Venezuelan terrorism | Cuba, Venezuela | Moderate | Some |
| 1964 | Panama Canal Zone | Panama, US | Insignificant | Some |
| 1965 | Dominican intervention | Dominican Republic, US | Low | Moderate |
| 1967-68 | Che Guevara | Bolivia, Chile, Cuba | Insignificant | Some |
| 1969-76 | Football war | El Salvador, Honduras | Low | Great |
| 1970-71 | American tuna boats | Ecuador, US | Insignificant | Some |
| 1974- | Chilean repression | Chile, all others | Moderate | Some |
| 1978-79 | Sandinista revolt | Nicaragua, Costa Rica | High | Some |
| 1978 | Beagle Channel | Chile, Argentina | Very low | Some |
| 1979 | Panama Canal tolls* | US, several others | Insignificant | None |
| 1980 | Bolivian coups* | Bolivia, Andean Pact | Insignificant | None |
| 1981 | Peru-Ecuador border 2 | Peru, Ecuador | Insignficant | Some |
| 1983- | Anti-Sandinista revolt—south | Costa Rica, Nicaragua | Low | None |
| 1983 | Grenada invasion | US, Grenada | Low | None |

## DISPUTES REFERRED TO THE ORGANIZATION OF AFRICAN UNITY (OAU)

| Date | Dispute | Parties | Intensity | Impact |
|---|---|---|---|---|
| 1963-67 | Somali borders | Somalia, Kenya, Ethiopia | Moderate | Some |
| 1963-66 | Ghanaian border | Ghana, Upper Volta | Very low | Some |
| 1963-66 | Algerian/Moroccan border | Algeria, Morocco | Moderate | Some |
| 1963-67 | Tutsi terrorism | Rwanda, Burundi | High | Some |
| 1963-67 | Affars and Issas | Somalia, Ethiopia (France) | Low | None |
| 1964-65 | Zaire civil war | Zaire, Burundi, Congo | Moderate | None |
| 1965-66 | Ghanaian subversion | Ghana, several francophone states | Insignificant | Some |
| 1966 | Ghanaian refugees | Guinea, Ghana | Insignificant | Great |
| 1967-70 | Biafra war | Nigeria, Biafra | High | None |
| 1967 | Battle of the hostages | Guinea, Ivory Coast | Insignificant | None |
| 1971-74 | Guinean repression | Guinea, Senegal | Very low | Some |
| 1972 | Burundi genocide | Burundi, Rwanda, Tanzania | High | Moderate |
| 1973 | Amin coup | Tanzania, Uganda | Low | Moderate |
| 1974-75 | Mali/Upper Volta border | Mali, Upper Volta | Insignificant | Great |
| 1974-79 | Ogaden war | Somalia, Ethiopia (USSR, Cuba) | High | Some |
| 1974- | Angola civil war | Angolan factions (South Africa, Cuba, USSR, China) | High | None |
| 1975-77 | Benin coup | Benin, Togo, Gabon, Morocco | Very low | Moderate |

Appendix A (continued): OAU

| Date | Dispute | Parties | Intensity | Impact |
|---|---|---|---|---|
| 1975- | Eritrean independence | Ethiopia, Arab states | High | None |
| 1976 | Kenya/Uganda border | Kenya, Uganda | Insignificant | None |
| 1976- | Western Sahara war | Algeria, Morocco, Mauritania | High | None |
| 1977 | Sudan/Ethiopia border | Sudan, Ethiopia, Eritrean factions | Very low | Some |
| 1978-79 | Amin overthrow | Uganda, Tanzania | Moderate | None |
| 1978- | Chad civil war | Chad factions, Libya, Sudan, (France) | High | None |
| 1979-80 | Gafsa incident | Tunisia, Libya | Low | Some |
| 1980- | Ethiopian civil war | Ethiopian factions, Somalia, (USSR, Cuba), Sudan | High | None |
| 1981-83 | Cameroon border | Nigeria, Cameroon | Insignificant | None |
| 1983- | Aouzou strip | Chad, Libya | Low | None |

DISPUTES REFERRED TO THE COUNCIL OF EUROPE

| Date | Dispute | Parties | Intensity | Impact |
|---|---|---|---|---|
| 1950-55 | Status of Saar | France, West Germany | Very low | Some |
| 1956-59 | Cyprus decolonization | Greece, UK | Low | Some |
| 1960-69 | South Tyrol | Austria, Italy | Insignificant | None |
| 1968-71 | Greek tyranny | Greece, Denmark, Netherlands, et al. | Very low | None |
| 1971-76 | Irish Republican Army prisoners | Ireland, UK | Very low | Some |

## DISPUTES WITH MILITARY OPERATIONS NOT REFERRED TO MAJOR INTERNATIONAL ORGANIZATIONS

| Date | Dispute | Parties | Intensity | Outcome |
|---|---|---|---|---|
| 1945-47 | Indo-Pakistan independence | Congress Party, Muslim League, UK | Moderate | Mediation |
| 1945-49 | Chinese civil war | Kuomintang, Chinese Communists, US, USSR | Very high | One side wins |
| 1946-47 | Kurdistan | Kurds, Iran, Iraq | High | Peters out |
| 1946-54 | Vietnam independence | Vietnam, France | Very high | Mediation |
| 1947-50 | Mongolian border | China, Mongolia | Very low | One side wins |
| 1947-60 | Malagasy independence | Madagascar, France | High | One side wins |
| 1947-63 | Pakhtunistan | Afghanistan, Pakistan | Moderate | Unresolved |
| 1948-60 | Malayan revolt | Malay Communists, UK | Very high | One side wins |
| 1948-62 | French India | India, France | Moderate | One side wins |
| 1948-63 | Aden/Yemen border | Yemen, UK | Moderate | Peters out |
| 1949 | Syrian-Lebanese tensions | Syria, Lebanon | Very low | Peters out |
| 1949-52 | Bolivian exiles | Bolivia, Chile | Moderate | Peters out |
| 1950-54 | Cambodian independence | Cambodia, France | Moderate | One side wins |
| 1951-54 | Britain in Suez | Egypt, UK | High | Mediation |
| 1951-54 | C-47 shootdown | US, USSR | Insignificant | One side wins |
| 1953 | Czech air incident | US, USSR, Czechoslovakia | Insignificant | Negotiation |

Appendix A *(continued):* Not Referred

| Date | Dispute | Parties | Intensity | Outcome |
|---|---|---|---|---|
| 1953-54 | Laotian independence | Laos, France | Low | Mediation |
| 1953 | East German revolt | East Germany, USSR | Insignificant | One side wins |
| 1954-62 | Ladakh | China, India | Moderate | One side wins |
| 1955 | El Al air incident | Israel, US, UK, Bulgaria | Insignificant | Negotiation |
| 1955-72 | Naga-Mizo revolt | India, Burma, Pakistan | Moderate | One side wins |
| 1956-69 | Rann of Kutch | India, Pakistan | Low | Mediation |
| 1956-57 | Jordanian revolt | Jordan, Syria | Low | One side wins |
| 1956 | Polish October | Poland, USSR | Very low | One side wins |
| 1956-58 | Moroccan post-independence tensions | Morocco, France | Low | Negotiation |
| 1957-58 | Spanish Southern Protectorate | Morocco, Spain, France | Moderate | Negotiation |
| 1958 | Quemoy-Matsu | US, China, Taiwan | Very low | Peters out |
| 1958-59 | Mexican shrimp boats | Mexico, Guatemala | Insignificant | Negotiation |
| 1959-61 | Paraguayan exiles | Paraguay, Cuba, Argentina | Low | Peters out |
| 1959-64 | Malawi independence | UK, Malawi, Rhodesia | Moderate | Negotiation |
| 1959-61 | Nepalese border | China, India | Insignificant | Negotiation |
| 1960- | Sino-Soviet border | China, USSR | High | Unresolved |
| 1960-63 | Mali/Mauritania border | Mali, Mauritania | Insignificant | Mediation |

90  *Appendix A*

Appendix A *(continued):* Not Referred

| Date | Dispute | Parties | Intensity | Outcome |
|---|---|---|---|---|
| 1961-70 | Thai/Cambodian border | Thailand, Cambodia | Moderate | Unresolved |
| 1961-70 | Iraqi Kurdish revolt | Iraq, Iran, Turkey | High | Negotiation |
| 1961-62 | Berlin Wall | US, USSR | Very low | Peters out |
| 1962 | Soccer riots, | Gabon, Congo, Benin | Insignificant | Mediation |
| 1962 | Nam Tha crisis | Thailand, Laos, North Vietnam, US | Low | Mediation |
| 1962 | Sino-Indian war | India, China | High | One side wins |
| 1962 | Brunei revolt | UK, Malaysia, Indonesia | Very low | One side wins |
| 1963-75 | Laotian civil war | US, South Vietnam, Laos, North Vietnam | High | One side wins |
| 1963-65 | Lete Island | Nigeria, Benin | Insignificant | Mediation |
| 1963-72 | Sudan civil war | Sudan, Egypt, USSR | High | Mediation |
| 1965-66 | Chadian tensions | Chad, Sudan, Ghana | Low | Mediation |
| 1965- | Thai Communist revolt | Thailand, Laos, Vietnam | High | Unresolved |
| 1967- | Burmese Communist revolt | Burma, China | Moderate | Unresolved |
| 1968-75 | Surinam borders | Netherlands, Guyana | Insignificant | Peters out |
| 1969-73 | Rio de la Plata demarcation | Uruguay, Argentina | Very low | Negotiation |
| 1969- | Northern Ireland | UK, Ireland | High | Unresolved |
| 1970-75 | French nuclear tests | France, Australia, New Zealand, Peru | Very low | Mediation, ICJ[c] |
| 1972- | Moroccan fisheries | Morocco, Spain | Insignificant | Unresolved |

[c] International Court of Justice

Appendix A *(continued):* Not Referred

| Date | Dispute | Parties | Intensity | Outcome |
|---|---|---|---|---|
| 1972 | Corisco Bay Islands | Gabon, Equatorial Guinea | Insignificant | Mediation |
| 1972- | Moro rebellion | Philippines, Libya | High | Unresolved |
| 1973-75 | Vietnamese truce | South Vietnam, North Vietnam | High | One side wins |
| 1973- | Baluchistan | Pakistan, Afghanistan | Low | Unresolved |
| 1973- | South China Sea Islands | Philippines, China, Vietnam | Very low | Unresolved |
| 1974-75 | Iranian Kurdish revolt 1 | Iraq, Iran | Moderate | Negotiation |
| 1975-76 | Cod war | Iceland, UK | Very low | Mediation |
| 1975 | Thai/Laotian border | Thailand, Laos | Low | Negotiation |
| 1975 | Mayaguez seizure | Cambodia, US | Very low | One side wins |
| 1976-77 | Bangladesh exiles | India, Bangladesh | Insignificant | Peters out |
| 1977 | Shaba 1 | Zaire, Angola, Cuba | Very low | One side wins |
| 1977- | Omani border | Oman, United Arab Emirates | Insignificant | Peters out |
| 1978 | Shaba 2 | Zaire, Angola, Cuba, Morocco, France | Low | One side wins |
| 1978 | Larnaca rescue | Egypt, Cyprus | Very low | Peters out |
| 1979 | Iran border incursions | Afghanistan, Iran | Insignificant | Peters out |
| 1979 | Laos border incursions | China, Laos | Very low | Peters out |
| 1979- | Iranian Kurdish revolt 2 | Iran, Iraq | High | Unresolved |
| 1979- | Afghan/Pakistan border | Afghanistan, USSR, Pakistan | Very low | Unresolved |

## Appendix A (continued): Not Referred

| Date | Dispute | Parties | Intensity | Outcome |
|---|---|---|---|---|
| 1979-82 | Syrian missile crisis | Israel, Syria | Low | One side wins |
| 1979 | Mauritanian civil war | Mauritania, Algeria, Morocco | Very low | One side wins |
| 1979 | Bahaman patrol boat | Cuba, Bahamas | Insignificant | Negotiation |
| 1980 | North Korean warship | South Korea, North Korea | Very low | Peters out |
| 1980- | Thai border incursions | Thailand, Vietnam, Cambodian factions | Low | Unresolved |
| 1980 | Cuban tanker | Cuba, Morocco | Insignificant | Peters out |
| 1980 | Kuwait border posts | Kuwait, Iran | Insignificant | Negotiation |
| 1981 | Raid on Mozambique 1 | South Africa, Mozambique | Low | Peters out |
| 1981 | Korean air incident | North Korea, US | Insignificant | Peters out |
| 1981 | Jordan/Syria tensions | Jordan, Syria | Insignificant | Peters out |
| 1982 | West Irian revolt | Indonesia, Papua-New Guinea | Insignificant | Peters out |
| 1982- | Mizo rebellion | India, Bangladesh | Very low | Unresolved |
| 1982 | Haitian raid | Haiti, exiles, (US) | Insignificant | Negotiation |
| 1982 | Fisheries off Venezuela | Trinidad, Venezuela | Insignificant | Negotiation |
| 1982 | Raid into Zimbabwe | Zimbabwe, South Africa | Very low | Unresolved |
| 1982 | Raid into Botswana | Botswana, South Africa | Insignificant | Peters out |
| 1982 | Ogaden raids | Somalia, Ethiopia | Low | Unresolved |
| 1982-83 | Zambia border | Zaire, Zambia | Insignificant | Negotiation |

Appendix A *(continued):* Not Referred

| Date | Dispute | Parties | Intensity | Outcome |
|---|---|---|---|---|
| 1983 | Rangoon assassinations | Burma, North Korea, South Korea | Insignificant | Peters out |
| 1983 | Raid on Mozambique 2 | Mozambique, South Africa | Very low | Negotiation |
| 1983 | Eritreans in Sudan | Ethiopia, Sudan | Very low | Unresolved |
| 1983 | Lake Chad | Chad, Nigeria | Insignificant | Negotiation |
| 1983 | Zimbabwe revolt | Zimbabwe, Botswana | Insignificant | Negotiation |
| 1984 | Gulf tanker raids | Saudi Arabia, Iran, Kuwait | Very low | Unresolved |
| 1984 | Thai/Burma border | Thailand, Burma | Insignificant | Unresolved |
| 1984- | Libyan embassy in London | Libya, UK | Insignificant | Negotiation |
| 1984 | Algerian/Moroccan border | Algeria, Morocco | Insignificant | Negotiation |

# APPENDIX B

Table A. CORRELATES OF SUCCESS: UNITED NATIONS

Table B. SALIENCE OF UNITED NATIONS DISPUTES

Table C. GLOBAL CONTEXT OF UNITED NATIONS DISPUTES

Table D. MANAGEMENT OF UNITED NATIONS DISPUTES

Table E. CORRELATES OF GREAT SUCCESS BY ERA

Table F. CORRELATES OF LIMITED SUCCESS BY ERA

Table G. NONIMPLEMENTERS OF SUBSTANTIVE UNITED NATIONS DECISIONS

SOURCES USED IN CODING DISPUTES

## Table A

### CORRELATES OF SUCCESS: UNITED NATIONS
*(In percent; N = 137)*

|  | Cases | | Degree of Success | | |
| --- | --- | --- | --- | --- | --- |
| Correlate | Number | Percent of total | No success (N = 62) | Limited success (N = 42) | Great success (N = 33) |
| *Intensity* | | | | | |
| Insignificant, very low | 49 | 36% | 43% | 41% | 16% |
| Low, moderate | 43 | 31 | 58 | 16 | 26 |
| High, very high | 45 | 33 | 38 | 33 | 29 |
| *Type of warfare* | | | | | |
| None | 38 | 28 | 56 | 34 | 10 |
| Very limited | 65 | 47 | 40 | 35 | 25 |
| Support of diplomacy, defeat enemy | 34 | 25 | 56 | 18 | 26 |
| *Extent of spread* | | | | | |
| Bilateral | 42 | 31 | 40 | 31 | 29 |
| Local | 72 | 52 | 54 | 33 | 13 |
| Regional, global | 23 | 17 | 30 | 22 | 48 |
| *Type of issue* | | | | | |
| Colonial | 48 | 35 | 40 | 29 | 31 |
| Cold war | 17 | 12 | 63 | 25 | 12 |
| Other | 44 | 32 | 34 | 39 | 27 |
| Cold war—internal | 12 | 9 | 58 | 33 | 8 |
| Other—internal | 16 | 12 | 69 | 19 | 13 |
| *Consensus (N = 132)* | | | | | |
| None, narrow | 35 | 27 | 71 | 29 | 0 |
| Wide, very wide | 97 | 73 | 37 | 31 | 32 |

Appendix B

Table A *(continued)*

|  | Cases | | Degree of Success | | |
| --- | --- | --- | --- | --- | --- |
| Correlate | Number | Percent of total | No success (N = 62) | Limited success (N = 42) | Great success (N = 33) |
| *Alignment* | | | | | |
| One or more aligned | 87 | 63% | 53% | 23% | 26% |
| Same bloc, nonaligned | 50 | 37 | 34 | 44 | 22 |
| *Power of parties* | | | | | |
| Superpowers | 31 | 23 | 58 | 26 | 16 |
| Large powers | 40 | 29 | 48 | 25 | 27 |
| Middle powers | 29 | 21 | 34 | 37 | 29 |
| All others | 37 | 27 | 43 | 35 | 22 |
| *Type of decision* | | | | | |
| None | 34 | 25 | 71 | 21 | 8 |
| Weak | 30 | 22 | 60 | 34 | 6 |
| Strong | 73 | 53 | 29 | 34 | 37 |
| *Type of operation* | | | | | |
| None | 61 | 44 | 67 | 28 | 5 |
| Secretariat | 49 | 36 | 39 | 37 | 24 |
| Military | 27 | 20 | 11 | 26 | 63 |
| *Leadership* | | | | | |
| One superpower | 19 | 14 | 47 | 36 | 17 |
| Two superpowers | 5 | 4 | 20 | 20 | 60 |
| Large, middle powers | 21 | 15 | 52 | 19 | 29 |
| Small, smallest powers | 62 | 45 | 60 | 34 | 6 |
| Secretary-General | 30 | 22 | 17 | 37 | 46 |

Appendix B

## Table B

### SALIENCE OF UNITED NATIONS DISPUTES
*(In percent; N = 137)*

| Era | Number | Intensity Low[a] | Intensity High[b] | Warfare None | Warfare Low[c] | Warfare High[d] | Spread Bilateral | Spread Local | Spread Regional | Spread Global | Overall success |
|---|---|---|---|---|---|---|---|---|---|---|---|
| 1945-50 | 20 | 55% | 45% | 50% | 25% | 25% | 20% | 60% | 10% | 10% | 33% |
| 1951-55 | 12 | 83 | 17 | 25 | 67 | 8 | 42 | 42 | 16 | 0 | 24 |
| 1956-60 | 16 | 56 | 44 | 44 | 31 | 25 | 38 | 38 | 19 | 5 | 40 |
| 1961-65 | 26 | 54 | 46 | 19 | 65 | 15 | 38 | 46 | 12 | 4 | 19 |
| 1966-70 | 14 | 43 | 57 | 14 | 57 | 29 | 36 | 57 | 0 | 7 | 24 |
| 1971-75 | 12 | 58 | 42 | 33 | 42 | 25 | 42 | 42 | 8 | 8 | 16 |
| 1976-80 | 24 | 33 | 67 | 25 | 58 | 17 | 13 | 70 | 13 | 4 | 17 |
| 1981-84 | 13 | 69 | 31 | 8 | 61 | 31 | 31 | 54 | 0 | 15 | 18 |

[a]Insignificant, very low, low
[b]Moderate, high, very high
[c]Very limited, support diplomacy
[d]Defeat enemy

Table C

GLOBAL CONTEXT OF UNITED NATIONS DISPUTES
(In percent; N = 137)

| Era | Number | Type of Issue | | | | | | Power of Parties | | | | Overall success |
|---|---|---|---|---|---|---|---|---|---|---|---|---|
| | | Decolon-ization | Cold war | Other | Internal Cold war | Internal Other | Cold war alignment[a] | Super[b] | Large[c] | Middle[d] | Other[e] | |
| 1945-50 | 20 | 35% | 35% | 15% | 10% | 5% | 70% | 45% | 30% | 15% | 10% | 33% |
| 1951-55 | 12 | 42 | 33 | 17 | 8 | 0 | 92 | 33 | 33 | 17 | 17 | 24 |
| 1956-60 | 16 | 37 | 6 | 31 | 13 | 13 | 75 | 19 | 37 | 13 | 31 | 40 |
| 1961-65 | 26 | 54 | 4 | 19 | 4 | 19 | 77 | 15 | 42 | 23 | 19 | 19 |
| 1966-70 | 14 | 36 | 7 | 43 | 7 | 7 | 71 | 14 | 21 | 21 | 43 | 24 |
| 1971-75 | 12 | 25 | 0 | 41 | 17 | 17 | 50 | 25 | 17 | 25 | 33 | 16 |
| 1976-80 | 24 | 25 | 0 | 46 | 8 | 2 | 38 | 8 | 21 | 25 | 46 | 17 |
| 1981-84 | 13 | 15 | 23 | 54 | 8 | 0 | 69 | 38 | 8 | 38 | 15 | 8 |

[a] Parties members of opposing blocs; one aligned/other nonaligned
[b] Super v. super; super v. all lesser; large v. large
[c] Large v. all lesser
[d] Middle v. middle; middle v. all lesser
[e] All others

100   Appendix B

## Table D
### MANAGEMENT OF UNITED NATIONS DISPUTES
(In percent; N = 137)

| Era | Number | Decision | | | Operation | | | Leadership | | | | | Consensus | |
|---|---|---|---|---|---|---|---|---|---|---|---|---|---|---|
| | | Minimal discussion | No operation | Operation | None | Non-military | Military | One super-power | Two super-powers | Large | All others | Secretary-General/joint | None/narrow[a] | Wide[b] |
| 1945-50 | 20 | 30% | 5% | 65% | 35% | 30% | 35% | 50% | 15% | 15% | 15% | 5% | 40% | 60% |
| 1951-55 | 12 | 33 | 42 | 25 | 67 | 17 | 17 | 25 | 0 | 17 | 50 | 8 | 25 | 75 |
| 1956-60 | 16 | 13 | 25 | 62 | 44 | 31 | 25 | 0 | 0 | 0 | 50 | 50 | 25 | 75 |
| 1961-65 | 26 | 27 | 12 | 61 | 35 | 54 | 11 | 8 | 0 | 4 | 58 | 31 | 27 | 73 |
| 1966-70 | 14 | 21 | 21 | 57 | 28 | 57 | 14 | 7 | 7 | 7 | 43 | 36 | 14 | 86 |
| 1971-75 | 12 | 33 | 33 | 33 | 58 | 17 | 25 | 8 | 8 | 0 | 59 | 25 | 33 | 67 |
| 1976-80 | 24 | 8 | 38 | 54 | 46 | 42 | 13 | 4 | 0 | 0 | 79 | 17 | 21 | 79 |
| 1981-84 | 13 | 38 | 31 | 31 | 69 | 23 | 8 | 8 | 0 | 15 | 62 | 15 | 23 | 77 |

[a] No consensus; minimal constitutional requirement
[b] Large majority; near unanimity; unanimity

Table E

CORRELATES OF GREAT SUCCESS BY ERA
(N = 33)

| Variable | Era | | | | | | |
|---|---|---|---|---|---|---|---|
| | 1945-50 (N = 8) | 1951-55 (N = 3) | 1956-60 (N = 6) | 1961-65 (N = 5) | 1966-70 (N = 4) | 1971-75 (N = 3) | 1976-80 (N = 3) | 1981-84 (N = 0) |
| Intensity | High | High | Low | Moderate | High | -- | Insignificant | -- |
| Type of warfare | Defeat enemy | Support diplomacy | Defeat enemy | Support diplomacy | Defeat enemy | Defeat enemy | -- | -- |
| Extent of spread | Bilateral | Bilateral | Regional, global | Regional, global | Local | Bilateral | -- | -- |
| Type of issue | Decolonization | -- | Decolonization | Decolonization | Other | Other | Other | -- |
| Cold war alignment | Aligned | Aligned | Aligned | Nonaligned | Nonaligned | Nonaligned | -- | -- |
| Power of parties | Super | -- | Large | Large | Large | Small | -- | -- |
| Type of decision | Strong | Strong | Strong | Strong | Strong | Strong | Strong | -- |
| Type of operation | Large | Large | Large | Small | Large | Large | -- | -- |
| Leadership | Super | -- | Secretary-General | Secretary-General | Secretary-General | Secretary-General | Small | -- |
| Consensus | Wide | Wide | Wide | Wide | Wide | Wide | Wide | -- |

NOTE: Codings made by selecting only subvariables that scored a minimum of 33 percent per era. Dashes reflect a distribution when no single subvariable scored 33 percent or when there were ties.

## Appendix B

Table F

CORRELATES OF LIMITED SUCCESS BY ERA
($N = 42$)

| Variable | 1945-50 ($N=5$) | 1951-55 ($N=1$) | 1956-60 ($N=6$) | 1961-65 ($N=5$) | 1966-70 ($N=5$) | 1971-75 ($N=2$) | 1976-80 ($N=13$) | 1981-84 ($N=5$) |
|---|---|---|---|---|---|---|---|---|
| Intensity | -- | -- | -- | Insignificant | Very low | Moderate | High | Insignificant |
| Type of warfare | Support diplomacy | -- | None | Limited | None/limited | -- | None/limited | Limited |
| Extent of spread | Local | -- | Local | Bilateral | Bilateral | Bilateral | Local | Local |
| Type of issue | Cold war | -- | Other | Decolonization | Other | -- | Other | Other |
| Cold war alignment | Nonaligned | -- | -- | Nonaligned | Aligned | -- | Nonaligned | Aligned |
| Power of parties | Large | -- | Small | Large | -- | -- | Small | Middle |
| Type of decision | Strong | -- | -- | Weak | Strong | -- | Strong | Weak |
| Type of operation | -- | -- | None | None | Small | -- | Small | None |
| Leadership | Super (1) | -- | Small | -- | -- | -- | Small | Small |
| Consensus | Wide | -- | -- | Wide | Wide | -- | Wide | Wide |

NOTE: Codings made by selecting only subvariables that scored a minimum of 33 percent per era. Dashes reflect a distribution when no single subvariable scored 33 percent or when there were ties.

## Table G

### NONIMPLEMENTERS OF SUBSTANTIVE UNITED NATIONS DECISIONS
*(In percent; N = 53)*

| Era | Number | Unimplemented decisions as percent of all decisions | Alignment | | | | Issue | | |
|---|---|---|---|---|---|---|---|---|---|
| | | | Super-power | Ally of super-power | Non-ally: large, middle | Non-ally: small, smallest | Cold war | Decolon-ization | Other |
| 1945-50 | 5 | 36% | 40% | 20% | 40% | 0 | 40% | 20% | 40% |
| 1951-55 | 4 | 50 | 0 | 100 | 0 | 0 | 0 | 75 | 25 |
| 1956-60 | 3 | 30 | 33 | 67 | 0 | 0 | 67 | 0 | 33 |
| 1961-65 | 11 | 58 | 9 | 82 | 9 | 0 | 9 | 55 | 36 |
| 1966-70 | 6 | 55 | 0 | 100 | 0 | 0 | 0 | 50 | 50 |
| 1971-75 | 5 | 71 | 20 | 40 | 20 | 20 | 20 | 40 | 40 |
| 1976-80 | 13 | 59 | 15 | 38 | 15 | 31 | 8 | 31 | 62 |
| 1981-84 | 6 | 75 | 33 | 50 | 17 | 0 | 33 | 33 | 33 |

*NOTE:* The cases are confined to instances of UN decisions in which specific acts of compliance were requested of the disputants. The figure for the most recent era is always highest; it normally goes down later.

## SOURCES USED IN CODING DISPUTES

*Africa Contemporary Record* (London)

*Africa Research Bulletin* (Exeter)

*Afrique Contemporaine* (Paris)

*Asian Recorder* (New Delhi)

*Asian Research Bulletin* (Hong Kong)

*Facts on File* (New York)

*Far Eastern Economic Review* (Hong Kong)

*Keesing's Contemporary Archives* (London)

*Middle East Journal* (Washington, D.C.)

*Latin American Regional Report* (London)

*New York Times*

*United Nations Monthly Chronicle* (New York)

**Organization of American States,** *Proceedings of General Assembly Permanent Council, Summary of Decisions*

*West Africa* (London)

ERNST B. HAAS is Robson Professor of Political Science at the University of California at Berkeley. Director of the Institute of International Studies at Berkeley from 1969 to 1973, his publications include *Scientists and World Order: The Uses of Technical Knowledge in International Organizations* (with Mary Pat Williams and Don Babai) (1977), *Human Rights and International Action* (1970), *Tangle of Hopes: American Commitments and World Order* (1969), *Beyond the Nation State: Functionalism and International Organization* (1964), *The Uniting of Europe* (1958) and *Dynamics of International Relations* (with A. S. Whiting) (1956).